THE INVENTION OF THE TELEGRAPH AND TELEPHONE IN AMERICAN HISTORY

The In American History Series

In
AMERICAN
HISTORY

THE INVENTION OF THE TELEGRAPH AND TELEPHONE IN AMERICAN HISTORY

Anita Louise McCormick

Enslow Publishers, Inc.

40 Industrial Road   PO Box 38
Box 398   Aldershot
Berkeley Heights, NJ 07922   Hants GU12 6BP
USA   UK

http://www.enslow.com

Library of Congress Cataloging-in-Publication Data

McCormick, Anita Louise.
    The invention of the telegraph and telephone in American history /
Anita Louise McCormick.
        v. cm. — (In American history)
        Includes bibliographical references and index.
        Contents: Alexander Graham Bell invents the telephone — Learning
about the power of electricity — Samuel Morse invents the telegraph —
How the telegraph changed America — The telephone enters American
life —Telecommunications connect America.
        ISBN 0-7660-1841-5
        1. Telegraph—United States—History—Juvenile literature.
2. Telephone—United States—History—Juvenile literature. [1. Telegraph.
2. Telephone. 3. Communication—History.] I. Title. II. Series.
TK5265.M35 2003
384.1'0973—dc21

                                                2003003707

Printed in the United States of America

10 9 8 7 6 5 4 3 2 1

To Our Readers: We have done our best to make sure all Internet Addresses in
this book were active and appropriate when we went to press. However, the
author and the publisher have no control over and assume no liability for the
material available on those Internet sites or on other Web sites they may link to.
Any comments or suggestions can be sent by e-mail to comments@enslow.com or
to the address on the back cover.

Illustration Credits: Carol Belanger Grafton, *Ready-to-Use Authentic
Civil War Illustrations: 245 Different Copyright-Free Designs Printed One
Side* (New York: Dover Publications, Inc., 1995), p. 65; Clipart.com,
pp. 6, 36; © Corel Corporation, p. 44; The Denver Public Library,
Western History Collection, p. 94; Digital Imagery® copyright 1999
Photodisc, Inc., p. 111, 112; Engraving by George R. Hall, reproduced
from the *Dictionary of American Portraits*, published by Dover
Publications, Inc., in 1967, p. 17; Enslow Publishers, Inc., pp. 32, 40;
John Grafton, *The American West in the Nineteenth Century*, (New York:
Dover Publications, Inc., 1992), p. 49; National Archives and Records
Administration, pp. 15, 61, 66, 71, 75; Reproduced from the Collections
of the Library of Congress, pp. 12, 25, 50, 52, 59, 78, 86, 87, 92, 97,
100, 109; Reproduced from the *Dictionary of American Portraits,* published by Dover Publications, Inc., in 1967, pp. 9, 56; U.S. Department
of Interior, National Park Service, Edison National Historic Site, p. 58.

Cover Illustration: Reproduced from the Collections of the Library of
Congress

★ CONTENTS ★

In 1892, Alexander Graham Bell demonstrated the telephone at the opening of a long distance line between New York and Chicago.

A New Invention

On June 2, 1875, Alexander Graham Bell and his assistant, Thomas A. Watson, were busy in their workshop in Boston, Massachusetts. The men were trying to invent a harmonic telegraph. This machine would send several telegram messages over a wire at the same time. (The regular telegraph provided a way to electrically send messages called telegrams.) If the men succeeded, it would mark a big improvement in telegraph service.

The transmitting device of the machine was in one room, and the receiver was in another. In order for the device to operate, metal strips in the harmonic telegraph had to vibrate at different frequencies. (Frequency is the rate of vibration of a sound wave.) If Bell's invention worked, each frequency the machine produced could be used to send a different message.

While Bell and Watson were testing the machine, Bell pressed the transmitter's key to make a strip in the device's receiver in Watson's room vibrate. But the strip was stuck to a magnet and did not move. Bell asked Watson to pluck the strip. This could free the strip and allow it to vibrate as it should.

Watson followed Bell's suggestion. However, when he plucked the metal strip in the receiver, a similar strip in Bell's transmitter did something surprising. It not only vibrated, but made a complex sound wave much like a musical note.

Bell and Watson repeated this experiment over and over again. Every time, they had the same results. This proved it was possible to use electric energy to transmit sound waves through a wire. If a simple sound like that created by Watson's metal strip could be transmitted, Bell and Watson wondered, could transmitting the human voice by means of electricity be far behind?

Both men were excited about this new discovery. It was the breakthrough Bell needed in his effort to invent the telephone. A telephone would transmit actual speech, while Bell's harmonic telegraph could only send and receive brief sounds.

Later that day, Bell wrote a letter to Gardiner Greene Hubbard. Hubbard was one of Bell's business partners and investors. In the letter, Bell told Hubbard that he had made an exciting discovery.

Working With Deaf Children

Alexander Bell was born in Edinburgh, Scotland, in 1847. Alexander's father worked with deaf students. Alexander also became interested in helping deaf people learn to speak. When he attended University College in London, England, he studied how the mouth, throat, and ears work together to make speech possible.

In June 1875, Alexander Graham Bell made a breakthrough in his effort to invent the telephone while he was trying to invent a harmonic telegraph.

In the late 1800s, tuberculosis was a serious problem in the British Isles. Alexander's younger and older brothers died of the disease. His father thought Canada was a healthier place to live, so he decided to move the family there. The Bells arrived on August 1, 1870.

Bell's father was already known as a speech teacher of the deaf in North America. He had lectured in the United States, and many people wanted to know more about his teaching methods. Alexander Graham Bell received an offer to work at a school for the deaf in Boston in 1871, so he moved there.

In 1873, Alexander Graham Bell became a professor at Boston University. He also began to teach students in private. His salary made it possible for him to buy some equipment he needed to build a harmonic telegraph. This would be a big improvement over the existing telegraph system, where only one message at a time could be sent.

Bell also had another invention in mind—a device that could pick up sounds and translate them into written symbols. The "phonautograph," as Bell named it, could be used to help deaf people learn to speak more clearly. It made a written image of their voice, allowing them to practice on their own and watch their improvement. In the summer of 1874, Bell made a working model of the phonautograph. He used an eardrum taken from a dead man for the part of the device that responded to sound.

While he was working with the phonautograph, Bell came upon a new idea. He wondered if a membrane similar to the eardrum could be used to translate the airwaves made by human speech into an electric current. Bell believed that once these waves were represented by an electric current, they could travel through wires and be picked up by a receiver at the other end. This was the beginning of Bell's idea for a telephone.

Setting Up Shop

When Bell needed more money to carry out his experiments, he looked for investors. These investors were people who believed in Bell's inventions enough to lend him money in hopes of eventually making a profit themselves. Gardiner Greene Hubbard was not only an investor, but also a lawyer. Hubbard checked through the paperwork at the United States Patent Office to make sure that nothing similar to the harmonic telegraph had already been invented. When he returned, he offered Bell money for his experiments. In exchange, he wanted some of the profits once the invention was successful. Thomas Sanders, a leather salesman who lived in the Boston area, also wanted to invest in the idea. Bell and his investors formed the Bell Patent Association in February 1875.

Bell carried out his experiments at Charles Williams's electrical shop on 109 Court Street in Boston. With money from his investors, Bell was able to hire an assistant, Thomas A. Watson, to help him with his work. Watson was good at making the parts that Bell needed for his experiments.

Telegraph Vs. Telephone

Bell's investors wanted him to focus his attention on inventing a harmonic telegraph. While Bell was interested in this project, his main ambition was to invent an electric device that could transmit the human voice over a wire—the telephone.

One night when they were relaxing from their work on the harmonic telegraph, Bell said, "Watson, I want to tell you of another idea I have, which I think will surprise you. . . . If I could make a current of electricity vary in intensity, precisely as the air varies in density during the production of a sound, I should be able to transmit speech telegraphically."[1]

The telephone and telegraph were different in one important way. With the telegraph, messages were sent by switching on and off the electrical current that traveled through the wire. These pulses of electricity

Alexander Graham Bell's main ambition was to invent the telephone. This model of Bell's first telephone is a duplicate.

were printed as a combination of dots and dashes, which could be translated by telegraph operators into letters and numbers. But the telephone worked under a different system. The electric current was always on, and the human voice and other sounds could be relayed over the telephone line by varying the strength of the electric current.

Bell's discovery of the telephone was the beginning of a brand-new industry. However, his invention was preceded by another amazing device—the telegraph. And before either invention could be conceived, people first had to learn about the power of electricity.

Until the telephone and telegraph were invented, long-distance communication was very slow. Most people had to write and send a letter to communicate over long distances. Many days, weeks, or even months often passed before letters reached their destinations. The mail moved no faster than the horses, steamships, or trains that carried it.

LEARNING ABOUT THE POWER OF ELECTRICITY

Sometimes, especially in the far West, the United States Postal Service and other messenger services did not transport letters during the winter. People in the West had to wait until the snow melted enough for horses and wagons to safely travel through the mountains.

In the early 1800s, a few European governments were using visual signaling systems to relay important messages. When enough tall towers had been set up, visual signaling could be used to relay messages hundreds of miles. That system was the fastest means of communication at the time. But it was limited to line-of-sight communications, and was only useful during daylight hours.

The United States would benefit from a rapid form of communication. Banks, businesses, newspapers, and government agencies all wanted to hear important news before their competition. Families and friends had to wait for weeks to hear from distant loved ones.

A few scientists thought that electricity could one day be used to improve communication. However, before such a system could be built, scientists and inventors had to learn more about electricity and how to control it. Until then, people had to wait patiently for the information they wanted to arrive.

Benjamin Franklin's Experiments With Electricity

Today, Benjamin Franklin is remembered mostly as an American statesman. But during his lifetime, Franklin had a worldwide reputation as a scientist who had a keen interest in electricity.

Franklin believed that lightning was produced by huge charges of electric current that gathered in storm clouds. So in June 1752, when a thunderstorm approached, he decided to test this theory. Franklin used a kite to lift a metal key into the storm. The kite became electrically charged and Franklin concluded that his theory was correct. (Lightning did not actually strike the kite.)

Even while Franklin was doing this experiment, he was aware that lightning strikes could be very danger-ous. If lightning had struck the kite, Franklin could have been seriously hurt or killed. Many times, he had

In 1752, Benjamin Franklin conducted an experiment using a kite and a metal key, which helped prove that lightning was produced by charges of electric current in storm clouds.

seen the damage lightning strikes could do. Ben Franklin's interest in this issue later prompted him to invent lightning rods to help protect ships and buildings from lightning's destructive power. A lightning rod is a metal pole that is used to attract lightning away from the building or ship it might otherwise hit. These special rods then directed the electricity into the ground or the water.

Franklin's discoveries about electricity were so important that biographer Carl van Doren wrote, "Franklin found electricity a phenomenon, and left it a science."[1]

Benjamin Franklin's experiments and the work of other scientists and inventors around the world who followed him led to development of ideas and devices that made electrical communications possible.

Galvanism

Important discoveries in the field of electricity were also made in Europe. In the 1780s, Luigi Galvani, an

Italian physician, discovered that electricity could be produced by the chemical interaction between different metals and liquids. This type of electricity produced by a chemical action later came to be known as galvanism.

In 1799, Italian physicist Count Alessandro Volta took the next step when he invented the first practical battery. It converted chemical energy into electrical energy. Volta's first batteries were made with pieces of copper and zinc in acid. The volt, a unit of electrical measurement, was named after Volta.

Electricity and Magnetism

Danish physicist Hans Christian Oersted discovered the relationship between electricity and magnetism in 1820. His experiments proved that when a magnetic compass was held next to a wire carrying electric current, the needle would move at a right angle. This proved that electricity had an effect on the compass's magnet.

English scientist Michael Faraday was another pioneer in the field of electricity. In 1831, he discovered it was possible to produce electricity by moving a magnet inside a coil of wire. This way of producing electricity is called electromagnetic induction. Using his discovery, Faraday then built the world's first electric motor. Later, after doing more research, he discovered how to make a generator and transformer. A generator changes mechanical energy to electrical energy. A transformer can change the voltage, or force, of an electrical current that changes direction. These inventions are very important because they provide ways of making and adjusting electric power so it can be used by people for light and powering machines. Because of Faraday's many accomplishments, the farad, a measurement of electrical charge, was named after him.

John Tyndall, a scientist and friend of Faraday, said, "When an experimental result was obtained by Faraday it was instantly enlarged by his imagination. I am acquainted with no mind whose power and suddenness of expansion at the touch of new physical truth could be ranked with his."[2]

Joseph Henry Invents the Electromagnet

Joseph Henry is one of the best-known American scientists of the 1800s. He was an expert in the power of electricity. Henry started his work with electromagnets in 1827. An electromagnet is a magnet that is created when an electric current flows through a wire. Henry invented a new type of electromagnet that was

Joseph Henry was a notable American physicist and a pioneer in the scientific field of electromagnetism.

very powerful. He increased the strength of the electromagnet by tightly wrapping insulated wire around the magnet many times. In 1829, he demonstrated an electromagnet that had four hundred turns of insulated wire. This was quite a strong magnet at the time. During the 1830s, Henry held demonstrations that showed how an electromagnet could create enough electricity to ring a small bell. For the first time, electromagnets could be built that were able to perform work at a distance.

Henry also invented the first motor that operated by means of electricity. Henry's electric motors and electromagnetic relays would eventually play an important role in the invention of the telegraph.

The Stage Is Set for the Telegraph

Henry, Franklin, Faraday, Galvani, Volta, Oersted, and other scientists published information about their experiments in the new field of electrical science. This information enabled other scientists and inventors to use the pioneers' theories to devise their own experiments.

Every time new research in the field of electricity was published, it sparked ideas in other scientists and inventors for yet more experiments. The work of these scientists and inventors continually built up a base of knowledge about electricity and how it could be used. Much of this information proved helpful to Samuel Morse, inventor of the telegraph.

On April 27, 1791, Samuel Morse was born in Charlestown, Massachusetts. His father, Jedidiah Morse, was a minister and a friend of George Washington, the first president of the United States.

SAMUEL MORSE INVENTS THE TELEGRAPH

Samuel first became interested in electricity when he was a teenager. At the time, scientists were just beginning to learn about electricity and what it could do. The science of electricity was still in the experimental stage. Scientists and inventors often debated the properties of electricity, and some had carried out experiments. But the American public had yet to see the power of electricity put to practical use.

Morse the Artist

While Samuel was still attending school, he worked part time as a bookseller. This provided him with a small income. But Samuel's goal was to be a famous painter. So he convinced his parents to give him the money he needed to travel to Europe and study art. In

June 1811, Samuel Morse boarded the ship *Sully* for a twenty-two-day ocean voyage from New York to London, England.

Morse did well in art school and returned home to Boston, excited to start his new career as a painter. But few people in Massachusetts were interested in buying Morse's paintings. Morse married Lucretia Walker in 1818. Over the next few years they had three children: Susan, born in 1819; Charles, born in 1823; and James, born in 1825. Soon after he was married, Morse realized he was not earning enough money to support a family. Lucretia and their children had to live with Morse's parents while he traveled in search of people who were willing to pay for his paintings.

On February 8, 1825, Lucretia died of a heart attack. It took two days for the news to reach Morse. By the time he was able to get home, Lucretia had already been buried. This incident is a good example of the need for more rapid communication during the early nineteenth century.

Even though he was not able to earn much money by painting, Morse did not give up on making a living as an artist. He and several other painters formed the National Academy, and Morse was chosen as the academy's first president. During that time, Morse also tried to promote a few inventions. But he could not find anyone to finance them. Morse worked hard to earn a living, but was not good at managing money.

Morse felt that if he had more training in art, he might still be able to make a name for himself. So in

November 1829, he sold nearly all his possessions and boarded a ship for Europe.

European Communication

While he was studying art in France, Morse had the opportunity to see how the French relayed important messages over long distances. Their visual message system, a type of communication called the optical telegraph, required that many tall towers be built. The towers were spaced about fifteen miles apart. To relay messages, someone had to climb to the top of the tower and operate a device that used mechanical arms to display a coded message for the person at the next tower to see. The message was repeated over and over again to make certain the next person in the relay had read it correctly. Then, that person would repeat the message for the operator in the next tower to read and relay.

The French system was the best of its time. The tall towers made it possible to relay urgent messages much

SOURCE DOCUMENT

THE INTERRUPTIONS DUE TO THE MACHINES BEING OUT OF ORDER ARE TERRIBLE: THEY HAPPEN AT ALMOST EVERY SESSION. THEY HAPPEN INVARIABLY JUST WHEN WE HAVE THE MOST IMPORTANT INFORMATION TO TRANSMIT . . .[1]

In a letter dated August 17, 1794, an operator at one of the towers describes the problems experienced during the early stages of the French optical telegraph.

faster than a person could walk or a horse could gallop. But the system had serious problems. It was useless at night. Also, fog, rain, and snow often filled the air, making it nearly impossible to communicate with the visual relay system.

The French system could only be used for line-of-sight communication. Mountains, tall trees, and other obstacles blocked communications unless extra towers were built to go around or over them. The French system had another drawback—it was not able to relay messages across large bodies of water.

Morse's Voyage Home Leads to New Ideas

In October 1832, Morse boarded the *Sully* again and started his journey home. Several passengers on the ship were interested in the new science of electricity. At that time, most people had heard of Benjamin Franklin's experience with electricity when he flew a kite during a thunderstorm. Also, it was generally known that a battery could produce a flow of current through a wire. But what else could the power of electricity do?

As Morse listened to the passengers' conversations, he began to wonder if electricity could somehow be used to relay messages. If it was possible to relay messages by means of electricity, this could lead to a whole new way of communicating.

Morse asked one passenger, Dr. Charles Thomas Jackson, if a wire's length slowed the movement of electric current. In the mid-1800s, the movement of electric current was not well understood. But based on his knowledge, Jackson did not think the length of a wire would make any difference.

This led Morse to conclude, "If this be so, and the presence of electricity can be made visible in any desired part of the circuit, I see no reason why intelligence [information] might not be instantly transmitted by electricity to any distance."[2]

During the remainder of his journey to the United States, Morse thought more and more about the possibilities of electric communication. He soon started sketching ideas for a device that could send and receive electrically transmitted messages through long pieces of wire.

Morse also worked out a code system of short and long signals—known as dots and dashes—that could be used to send messages. Each group of dots and dashes represented a letter or a number. A dot was made by connecting two pieces of metal and closing the circuit connection for an instant, then opening it again. A dash was made by closing the circuit for a slightly longer period. In Morse's telegraph code system, a dash was three times longer than a dot. This system would be improved later and would become known as Morse code.

After six weeks at sea, the *Sully* arrived in America. Before Morse left the ship, he said, "Well Captain, should you ever hear of the telegraph one of these days as the wonder of the world, remember the discovery was made on board the good ship *Sully*."[3] Morse told his brothers Sidney and Richard about his new invention. They were very excited about the idea, and thought it had a good chance of succeeding.

Morse Begins Work on the Telegraph

Upon his return to America, Samuel Morse immediately went to work building a model of his telegraph. He did not have many materials available. So he used a table, a picture frame, and melted pieces of lead to construct a model of his idea.

The telegraph worked, as Morse expected. But he still had a lot of work to do before the basic idea he demonstrated with this crude model could be used as a practical means of communication. Many problems still had to be solved. However, Morse had very little money and could not afford to promote his invention.

While he was experimenting with ideas for the telegraph, Morse took a job as a professor of art at the University of the City of New York. The university had recently opened, and it could not afford to pay Morse a high salary. So he ate and slept in the classroom where he taught.

Work on the telegraph went slowly. Morse did not have enough money to buy the reels of insulated wire he wanted for his experiments. So he bought shorter, less expensive pieces of wire and fastened them together. He then wrapped the wires with cotton thread. This insulated them and kept them from touching each other. Morse built many of the things he needed in his

While he experimented with ideas for the telegraph, Samuel Morse was also an artist. This self-portrait was painted in his late life.

work from parts of old clocks and frames and other discarded art equipment.

The telegraph Morse invented could transmit messages by way of electricity from one point to another. But he soon learned that Jackson's theory was wrong. When the receiver was placed too far away from the transmitter, the electric signal that carried the message became very weak or could not be received at all. This was one of the major problems Morse had to solve before the telegraph could be put to practical use.

Alfred Vail, a skilled mechanic whose father owned a machine shop, was the first investor to show an interest in Morse's work. Vail gave Morse money to fund his work and advice on his invention in exchange for a part of any possible profits.

Many of Morse's friends and associates thought his best chance at gaining wealth was through his work on the telegraph. But Morse had very little experience in science or electricity. Because of this, he did not know how to deal with many technical problems that came up in his work.

Morse's Rivals

While Morse was experimenting with the telegraph, he was not aware that other men were attempting to invent a similar means of communicating by electric signals. Professor Charles Wheatstone, a British physicist; William Fothergill Cooke, a British medical student with an interest in electricity; and the German scientist, Carl Friedrich Gauss, were already working on the problem before Morse boarded the *Sully* for his trip home from Europe.

Cooke and Wheatstone were working on the problem together. The British government rejected their idea for an electrical telegraph. But in the late 1830s, British railroad managers realized how important the invention was and put it into service.

Also, Morse was not the first person to think of using the pulse of electricity as a way to transmit messages. By the time Morse began experimenting with the telegraph, at least two other men had already come up with a code using long and short signals that could be used to transmit messages with electricity. Francis Bacon of England invented a code. And the Russian diplomat, Pavel Lvovitch Schilling, had developed a similar system. Morse's original idea was for each code to represent a number, which would then be translated into letters. But his business partner, Alfred Vail, suggested that he have the code represent letters, as well as numbers.

Morse Gains a New Business Partner

In 1836, Leonard Gale, a man who taught chemistry at the University of the City of New York, decided to help Morse fund his invention. Gale told Morse that a physicist at the College of New Jersey (now Princeton University), Joseph Henry, had invented an electromagnetic device that could be used to transmit sound.

Henry told Morse how to keep an electrical signal strong over a distance by using batteries along the telegraph wire. The batteries boosted the electric signal so it would not fade before it reached its final destination.

Finding a Way to Transmit Messages Through Wire

With the knowledge acquired from Henry, Morse and Gale continued to experiment with ideas for a telegraph. With each design they built, they tried transmitting messages over a wire Morse hung around his workroom.

To send messages over a telegraph line, Morse knew that the electrical current that passed through the line had to be altered in some way. The easiest way to do this was to open and close the circuit by means of a device such as a telegraph key that a person could press down. Morse also had to invent a piece of electrical equipment that could receive telegraph messages. Without such a device, an invention that transmitted messages by wire would be useless.

For the receiver, Morse used a magnetized piece of metal that clicked with every dot and dash that came through the wire. One early model of Morse's receiver employed a mechanical device to record messages. It used a pencil to record the dots and dashes that made up the coded messages on a strip of paper. Then, someone had to look at the paper, interpret the code, and write down the letters the dots and dashes represented. Later on, telegraphic messages were read and interpreted mostly by ear.

By the end of 1837, Morse and Gale were able to build a working model of an electromagnetic telegraph. Much of their idea was based on Joseph Henry's work. In early 1838, Morse held a public demonstration of the electric telegraph in Morristown, New Jersey. Several people came, but no one offered to lend Morse and his partners the money they needed to promote Morse's invention.

On January 24, 1839, Morse and Vail displayed the telegraph in New York City. The demonstration took place at the Geological Cabinet at New York University. Many reporters and scientists came to see the new invention.

From New York, Morse went to the Franklin Institute in Philadelphia, Pennsylvania. On February 8, he demonstrated the telegraph to the Committee of Arts and Sciences. His demonstration was so successful that he decided to take his telegraph to Washington, D.C., to convince the United States government to finance his invention.

SOURCE DOCUMENT

THE TELEGRAPH.—WE DID NOT WITNESS THE OPERATION OF PROFESSOR MORSE'S ELECTRO-MAGNETIC TELEGRAPH ON WEDNESDAY LAST, BUT WE LEARN THAT THE NUMEROUS COMPANY OF SCIENTIFIC PERSONS WHO WERE PRESENT PRONOUNCED IT ENTIRELY SUCCESSFUL. INTELLIGENCE WAS TRANSMITTED THROUGH A CIRCUIT OF TEN MILES, AND LEGIBLY WRITTEN AT THE EXTREMITY OF THE CIRCUIT.[4]

The New York University demonstration attracted the attention for which Morse had hoped. The January 29, 1839 issue of The Journal of Commerce *reported on the demonstration.*

Seeking Government Funding

By the late 1830s, some members of Congress had realized that the United States needed a better communications system. In the near future, sending messages by horse, steamship, or wagon train would be too slow to serve the economy of the quickly growing nation.

In 1837, Congress had asked inventors to submit ideas for a system that could relay messages more rapidly than horses or steamboats. One of their main goals at the time was to connect the financial leaders in New York City with the huge cotton market in New Orleans, Louisiana. Samuel Morse was the only inventor to suggest using an electric telegraph system for rapid communications.

Morse was thrilled when he was permitted to set up a demonstration of his telegraph in the Committee of Commerce's meeting room. This raised his hope of the government funding his invention. Morse wanted to build a telegraph line between two nearby cities to test his theory. But the United States was having economic problems. Even though some important people saw value in Morse's invention, Congress refused to approve any money for Morse.

After being rejected by his own government, Morse took his invention to Europe. When he went to England, Morse found that several other telegraph systems were already being used. As a result, the English government was not interested in funding his invention.

Morse then went on to Paris, France. There, he was able to show his electric telegraph to many important scientists. They thought his invention was wonderful, and stories about it soon spread throughout France.[5] Soon, important people from across the country came to witness the new machine. But even though the French scientists liked Morse's invention, their government would not finance his experiments.

Morse returned to America and continued his effort to get the United States government to fund his invention. He explained that his telegraph could connect the nation and speed communications for the government, businesses, and individuals.

Morse felt that the government would be more likely to fund his invention if Joseph Henry endorsed the project. Henry was already a respected scientist and professor. At Morse's request, Henry wrote a letter saying, "Science is now fully ripe for this application, and I have not the least doubt, if proper means be afforded, of the perfect success of the invention."[6] But still, Congress did not approve funding.

Obtaining a Patent

The telegraph system of Charles Wheatstone and William Cooke first went into operation in 1838. It was built along the British railways. While the Wheatstone and Cooke telegraph was operated by means of electricity, it used needles as a means of visual signaling. When a message came in, two of the five needles rotated on the receiving device and pointed to letters on a display.

Wheatstone and Cooke wanted to become partners with Morse in the American market. When Morse turned them down, Wheatstone and Cooke contacted the United States Patent Office and were issued a patent for their version of the telegraph.

Morse was not able to obtain a patent for his electric telegraph system from the United States Patent Office until June 20, 1840—eight days after Wheatstone and Cooke had obtained theirs. However, Morse's design was based on different technology. Because of this, the patent Wheatstone and Cooke obtained did not infringe on Morse's right to receive a patent of his own.

While working on getting a patent for his telegraph, Morse continued to paint, teach art, and work on several other inventions. Besides the telegraph, Morse popularized a new photographic process invented in France by Louis Daguerre. It was called daguerreo-type, and was one of the earliest forms of photography.

Promoting the Telegraph

Morse decided to promote his invention to potential investors by holding public demonstrations. To pre-pare for one demonstration, he bought two miles of

a= ● –	m= – –	y= – ● – –
b= – ● ● ●	n= – ●	z= – – ● ●
c= – ● – ●	o= – – –	1= ● – – – –
d= – ● ●	p= ● – – ●	2= ● ● – – –
e= ●	q= – – ● –	3= ● ● ● – –
f= ● ● – ●	r= ● – ●	4= ● ● ● ● –
g= – – ●	s= ● ● ●	5= ● ● ● ● ●
h= ● ● ● ●	t= –	6= – ● ● ● ●
i= ● ●	u= ● ● –	7= – – ● ● ●
j= ● – – –	v= ● ● ● –	8= – – – ● ●
k= – ● –	w= ● – –	9= – – – – ●
l= ● – ● ●	x= – ● ● –	0= – – – – –

Each telegraph message consisted of sets of dots and dashes. Each set corresponded to a letter of the alphabet or a number.

wire and insulated it by wrapping it in cotton, tar, and rubber. He then got in a rowboat and laid the wire across the New York harbor. He tested the equipment with telegraph operators at both ends of the cable, and everything worked.

In October 1842, Morse was ready to show off his invention. He ran a big ad in New York newspapers, inviting the public to see his telegraph in operation.

But the day after the ad ran, some fishermen ran across the cable. Not knowing what it was, they pulled it out of the water and cut it. Morse did not have time to prepare another cable before the scheduled demonstration, so he was forced to cancel it. When they found out they would not get to see the telegraph in operation, many people called Morse a liar and a fraud.

Back to Congress

Despite this setback, Morse continued to search for ways to fund this new system of communications. He believed the electric telegraph system he wanted to build should "contribute to the happiness of millions."[7]

In the fall of 1842, Morse wrote to a friend, "For nearly two years past, I have devoted all my time and scanty means, living on a mere pittance, denying myself all pleasures, and even necessary food, that I might have a sum to put my Telegraph into such a position before Congress as to insure success to the common enterprise."[8]

Morse returned to Washington, D.C., that December to once again ask Congress for the money he needed to put his telegraph into service. By then, Morse's idea for an electric telegraph had gained some interest in Congress. His hopes were high.

Francis O. J. "Fog" Smith, the chairman of the House Committee on Commerce, had invested money in Morse's invention and wanted to see it succeed. He convinced the committee to propose a bill granting Morse thirty thousand dollars to build a telegraph line between Washington, D.C., and Baltimore, Maryland, a distance of about forty miles.

Some congressmen, especially those from the industrial north, were in favor of the project. But most congressmen from the southern states, where the majority of people farmed to make a living, opposed the idea.[9]

Congress was occupied with the growing hostility between the North and South over the issue of slavery. Morse also had another problem. The majority of senators and congressmen of the time had no real knowledge of electricity. Very few had any idea of the great benefits rapid electrical communication could bring to the United States.

Even with recommendations from Fog Smith and Joseph Henry and other scientists and inventors, Morse and his idea for an electric telegraph were mocked in Congress. Several representatives tried to add amendments to the bill that would keep it from passing. One congressman said, "If we are going to spend money to develop the telegraph, I move that we also appropriate money to investigate mesmerism [hypnotism]."[10] Another congressman said, "We should also put up money to test Millerism,"[11] (Millerism was a belief that Jesus Christ would return in 1844.)

Despite the jokes, Morse did his best to get funding for the telegraph. He stayed to campaign for the bill until the last night of the Congressional session, February 23, 1843. By the time he left, his proposal had not even been presented.

Congress Passes the Telegraph Bill

The next morning, Annie Ellsworth—the daughter of Morse's friend, H. L. Ellsworth, the commissioner of patents—came to Morse's door with exciting news. In a surprise move, the House of Representatives had decided to bring up Morse's request just before midnight. It had passed by six votes: 89–83.[12] However, seventy members of Congress were so uncertain of what to do that they stayed in the cloakroom—a room used as a closet to hang coats—so they could avoid voting on the bill.[13] The Senate approved the bill a few days later, and President John Tyler then signed the bill into law.

Now that the Telegraph Bill had been approved, Morse could test his invention on a larger scale than ever before. Congress gave him two months to build a telegraph line between Baltimore, Maryland, and Washington, D.C.

The Baltimore & Ohio Railroad Company owned a train track between the two cities. So Samuel Morse decided to ask the railroad for permission to build his experimental telegraph line alongside of the train track. The Baltimore & Ohio Railroad Company agreed to Morse's plan, providing that the telegraph line could be built "without embarrassment to the operations of the company." The railroad company had one more condition—if the telegraph worked, they demanded the right to use it without cost.[14]

Morse and his people quickly went to work burying the telegraph line in the ground along a railroad

Morse demonstrates his telegraph to some curious onlookers.

track. When the project was almost finished, Morse discovered that workers had failed to insulate the telegraph line. Without insulation, a telegraph line buried in the ground was certain to fail because the ground would absorb the electric signals.

Only seven thousand of the thirty thousand dollars the United States government granted Morse to build the telegraph line remained. But that was enough for Morse and his crew to reinstall the telegraph wires on wooden poles alongside the railroad track.

Reporting on Political Conventions

In the spring of 1844, the two main political parties of the time, the Democrats and the Whigs, held their conventions in Baltimore, Maryland. They were to nominate candidates to run for president and vice president. Morse decided to use this opportunity to demonstrate the telegraph.

By May 1, 1844, when the Whigs held their convention, Morse's telegraph line had reached Annapolis Junction, Maryland. Alfred Vail, one of Morse's assistants, went to Annapolis Junction to meet the delegates at the train station and find out who had been nominated. Nearly everyone thought Henry Clay would be nominated for president, but no one knew who would be nominated for vice president. As soon as Vail learned that Theodore Frelinghuysen had been chosen, he sent the news to Morse in Washington, D.C., by telegraph.

When the convention delegates' train reached Washington, D.C., they came to the Capitol building with news of Clay and Frelinghuysen's nomination. The delegates were all astonished to learn Morse had already received the news by telegraph and had spread the word throughout the city.[15]

Later that month, the line between Washington and Baltimore was complete. Morse prepared to hold a demonstration of his telegraph for important political leaders in Washington. Morse told Annie Ellsworth that she could write the message he would send in the first official telegram between the two cities.

On May 24, 1844, Morse sat in the United States Supreme Court chamber in Washington, D.C., ready to demonstrate the new telegraph line. As Whig presidential nominee Henry Clay, former first lady Dolley Madison, and other important people watched, he tapped out a passage from the Bible that Annie Ellsworth had selected, "What hath God wrought?"

The electric signals that made up the message whizzed through the line. Almost as soon as he sent the dots and dashes, a telegraph operator in Baltimore received it and transmitted the message back to Morse to prove that it got there. With this demonstration, Morse was able to show an audience of influential people that his telegraph could actually relay messages over long distances.

SOURCE DOCUMENT

THE ELECTRIC TELEGRAPH IS CAPABLE OF DOING THE GREATEST SERVICE TO MANKIND, OR IT MAY DO THE GREATEST HARM.[16]

In this June 25, 1846 quote, Morse recognizes the potential power of the telegraph.

Profiting From the Telegraph

By 1845, Morse had attracted enough investors to form the Magnetic Telegraph Company. Their first project was to build a telegraph line from Baltimore, Maryland to Philadelphia, Pennsylvania, and New York. A year later, they expanded the system to include Boston, Massachusetts, and Buffalo, New York.

Morse tried to sell his patent for the telegraph to the United States Government for $100,000. But even though Morse had proved the telegraph worked, the government feared it would not make a profit and refused to buy it. After that, Morse decided to lease the right to use the telegraph to private businesses.

As a result, many different telegraph companies went into business throughout the eastern United States. Messages to a distant location often had to go through the lines of several telegraph companies before they reached their destinations.

As more and more telegraph lines were installed, the United States quickly began to change.

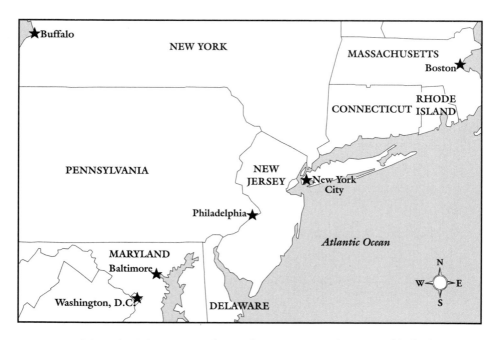

Morse's Magnetic Telegraph Company first established telegraph lines between the major cities of the Northeast. Throughout the mid- and late-nineteenth century, telegraph lines would spread across the country.

Such a network of wires . . . will one day connect together the ends of the earth, and, like the great nerves of the human body, unite in living sympathy all the far-scattered children of men.

—George Wilson,
Electricity and the Electric Telegraph, 1855[1]

HOW THE TELEGRAPH CHANGED AMERICA

From the time the first electric telegraph lines between cities were installed, communications began to change the way Americans worked and lived. Distance no longer separated the nation as it had in the past. To Americans living in the mid-1800s, the telegraph seemed as modern as lightning-speed Internet connections are to people today.

By the late 1840s, telegraph lines were being erected so quickly that no one could keep track of the construction. In 1848, one writer said:

> No schedule of telegraph lines can now be relied upon for a month in succession, as hundreds of miles [of wire] may be added in that space of time. It is anticipated that the whole of the populous parts of the United States will, within two or three years, be covered with net-work like a spider's web.[2]

By then, about two thousand miles of telegraph lines had been constructed.

In 1850, twenty telegraph companies had built over twelve thousand miles of telegraph line. By that year, the major cities and towns in the eastern part of the United States had telegraph service from at least one company. Individuals and businesses in large cities, such as New York, could select from up to a dozen telegraph services. In 1852, *Scientific American* wrote, "The spread of the Telegraph is about as wonderful of a thing as the noble invention itself."[3]

By 1854, nearly twenty-three thousand miles of telegraph lines were in use. There were more miles of telegraph lines than railroad tracks. The United States was well on the way to being connected.

Bringing the Telegraph to the West

In 1861, workers began the task of setting poles and stringing wires to connect California and the other western states and territories to the populated centers of the East. This was a difficult job, because few people lived in the West and supplies for the project were difficult to transport over such long distances.

One telegraph-line worker, Charley Brown, kept a diary of his team's progress. He documented how the men lived and worked, and problems they encountered along the way. Brown's team started their work in Julesburg and erected telegraph lines across the Wyoming Territory.

The team planned to install about twenty-four wooden telegraph poles per mile. They began the job on July 2, 1861, by setting fifteen poles and taking the telegraph wire across a river. Because few trees grow in the plains, some of the poles had to be transported from the distant locations where they were made.

By July 6, Brown's team had discovered that the telegraph poles they had to use "were crooked, knotty, and most of them good sized trees, dead, dry and brittle. We cut and piled eighteen. Getting such poles was very unsatisfactory, but we had to have them."[4]

Almost from the beginning, they ran into problems with the hostile environment. Extreme heat, a lack of drinking water, biting insects, and sharp cactus thorns made life difficult for the telegraph crew. In one July diary entry, Brown wrote, "The mosquitoes hung around and over the [Chimney Rock] station in great swarms. In all my experience on the Plains I have never seen these . . . pests in such numbers."[5]

Problems of the West

Building telegraph lines in the western states was only part of the job of connecting the nation. After the poles were up and the lines were connected, the next challenge was to keep the system in operation.

When a telegraph line in the East went out of service, it usually did not take long for a worker to find and repair the problem. But in the West, telegraph offices were often hundreds of miles apart. Finding and repairing problems on the western telegraph lines was time-consuming—and often dangerous—work.

Buffalo Knock Down Telegraph Poles

Some people feared that American Indians who were angry at whites for coming through their land would destroy telegraph poles and cut the lines. But in the beginning, buffalo proved to be a much more serious problem to the telegraph crews.

In the mid-1800s, large herds of buffalo still roamed the western plains. In areas where trees were scarce, buffalo used the telegraph poles to lean against

Herds of buffalo were a serious problem to telegraph crews. The animals would use telegraph poles to scratch their backs, knocking the poles down in the process.

and scratch their backs. Often, several buffalo would take turns rubbing against a pole until it became unstable and fell to the ground.

To discourage the buffalo, one supervisor, Ed Creighton, told his workers in the Wyoming Territory to drive spikes into the telegraph poles. But that approach failed because the buffalo had thick fur and tough skin. They seemed to enjoy leaning against the spiked poles even more than the regular poles! So the spikes had to be removed.

For a while, telegraph workers in the West had to deal with the task of resetting the poles the buffalo pushed over. Soon, however, the number of buffalo were greatly reduced by hunters.

American Indians and the Telegraph

When American Indians saw the telegraph lines being built through their territory, they usually left the workers alone. Some were curious about the project. Most telegraph crews did everything they could to maintain friendly relations.

On several occasions, the workers demonstrated the telegraph to tribal chiefs. A group of chiefs at one station would tell the telegraph operator a story, and he would relay it to another group of chiefs at a nearby station. The chiefs were impressed.

The American Indians' only means of rapid communication were beating drums, smoke signals, and messengers on horseback. They viewed the telegraph as the white man's effort to do the same. But even after the demonstrations, American Indians did not always realize the wires and poles that were being built would one day carry news instantly from one part of the country to another.

In the mid-1860s, relations between the telegraph companies and American Indians began to change. The Civil War between the Union Army of the North and the Confederate Army of the South was at its peak. The Union Army called many men who had guarded the telegraph lines and stations into service. Some American Indians, who by then had experienced poor treatment by whites, saw the weakness and began attacking telegraph stations. Many telegraph stations in Colorado, Nebraska, and Wyoming were raided.

The Union Army was angry. They decided to punish the American Indians for these attacks. So on November 29, 1864, nearly nine hundred soldiers were sent against the Cheyenne and Arapaho camps near Sand Creek in Colorado. The Union Army killed almost three hundred American Indians.

When word spread about the attack, some American Indian tribes in the West grew even more determined to destroy every telegraph line they could. The Army sent in more troops to prevent this from happening. But even when telegraph stations were well guarded, American Indians could disrupt the service by tearing down telegraph lines in isolated areas.

The Northern Lights Disrupt Telegraph Service

The telegraph company owners expected to have problems with weather, attacks by angry American Indians, and disruptions by opposing sides during the Civil War. However, they encountered one problem that no one had anticipated.

The Aurora Borealis, also known as the Northern Lights, is caused by an electrical charge in the atmosphere originating from the sun. This phenomenon caused severe electrical interference, making it impossible for telegraph operators or automatic printers to read Morse code. It put entire sections of the telegraph system out of operation.

An Aurora Borealis took place on August 28, 1859. It lit up the northern skies and disrupted telegraph service throughout northern parts of the United States and Canada. The electrical charges from the Northern Lights were so strong that even messages on telegraph lines less than twenty miles long were severely disrupted. Even before the Aurora Borealis was visible in the night sky, telegraph operators who worked the telegraph line between Boston and New Bedford, Massachusetts, were having serious problems communicating.

The superintendent of the Canadian telegraph lines, Mrs. O. S. Wood, described the incident this way:

> I never, in my experience of 15 years in the working of telegraph lines, witnessed anything like the extraordinary effect of the aurora borealis, between

Quebec and Father's Point, last night. The line was in most perfect order, and well-skilled operators worked incessantly from 8:00 last evening till 1:00 this morning, to get over, in even a tolerably intelligible form, about 400 words of the steamer Indian's report for the press; but at the latter hour, so completely were the wires under the influence of the aurora borealis, that it was found utterly impossible to communicate between the telegraph stations, and the line was closed for the night.[6]

The Telegraph and the Railroads

Despite all the problems in the West, the telegraph was there to stay. As more Americans moved to the West in search of new opportunities, telegraph lines were usually built alongside the railroads. Having telegraph service helped the railroads in several ways. They could telegraph ahead if there was a change of schedule. They also could prevent wrecks by letting other stations know about an approaching train or problems with the track.

Telegraph operators along the line could inform people in nearby towns about crimes soon after they were committed. If a train had been robbed or attacked, authorities in the area could be put on alert. Sometimes, law enforcement officials were able to arrest robbers and other criminals because a telegraph operator had relayed a description to the next town before the criminal arrived.

In the late 1800s, many railroad stations in the United States had a telegraph office that handled

As the United States expanded westward, more and more railroads were created. Telegraph lines were usually built alongside these railroads, as seen in this drawing.

messages for many private message companies, as well as the railroad. In small train stations, one person often acted both as a telegraph operator and station agent.

Western Union

By 1860, the telegraph system had grown tremendously. Over fifty thousand miles of telegraph lines had been constructed in the United States. Already, a few large telegraph companies, including the American Telegraph Company and Western Union, were starting to dominate the business.

Hiram Sibley, the founder of Western Union, got into the telegraph business by combining many small telegraph companies. The Mississippi Printing and Telegraph Company was his first venture into the business. Sibley was the president of Western Union from 1856 to 1869. By the time Sibley retired, Western

Some railroad stations in the 1800s had telegraph offices where one person acted both as telegraph operator and station agent.

Union had about four thousand telegraph offices across the United States.

New Job Opportunities

As the telegraph industry grew, telegraph companies employed thousands of people across the nation. Men were hired to construct and maintain the growing network of telegraph lines that now crossed America.

In 1860, the census listed approximately two thousand men as being employed as telegraph operators. The 1860 census did not separate men and women, but it is estimated that around one hundred women worked as telegraph operators at the time. When Virginia Penny wrote *How Women Can Make Money* in 1870, she said about fifty women living in the Northeast worked for the New York and Boston Magnetic Telegraph Company. By then, many other telegraph companies across the nation also employed women.[7]

Since the early years of the telegraph, women had been employed as operators. Receiving and sending messages in Morse code was one of the few technical jobs open to women at the time.

Sarah G. Bagley, the founder of the Lowell Female Labor Reform Association, was one of the first women to be hired as a telegraph operator. Bagley took the job as a telegraph operator in Lowell, Massachusetts, in 1846. By then, she was already known as a newspaper editor and women's rights supporter.

Western Union quickly became a top telegraph company, employing large numbers of people.

Once the network was in place, both men and women were trained to send and receive Morse code so they could take jobs at telegraph stations. In the mid-1800s, job opportunities for women were very limited. So taking a job as a telegraph operator gave more women a chance to earn an income for themselves and their families.

Ma Kiley

One of the most famous woman telegraph operators in the United States was Ma Kiley. In 1880, she was born Mattie Collins Brite in Atacosa County, Texas. She worked as a telegraph operator for forty years. Ma Kiley learned Morse code as a way to make a living after fleeing an abusive husband. Most of her jobs were in remote locations. During her time as a telegraph operator, she worked at railroad telegraph stations, Western Union, and the Postal Telegraph from northern Mexico to Saskatchewan, Canada. She retired at the age of sixty-two in 1942.

Later in her life, Ma Kiley wrote "The Bug and I," a series of articles published by *Railroad Magazine* in 1950. ("Bug" is a slang word for a telegraph key.) In one article, she wrote about the difference in pay between men and women telegraph operators in 1907:

> [The boss] informed me that he paid the men sixty-five dollars and the women forty and fifty, but I soon told him this woman didn't work for any such salary. He then said, "You must think you are some operator!" I told him I didn't need to think anything at all about it, I knew I was. Then, thinking to frighten me, he sat me down to a duplex, which is a wire used for sending and receiving at the same time. I copied everything that came over with a pencil, and when I finished all the operators were standing around with their mouths wide open that was a feat none of them had ever tackled. I was hired at sixty-five dollars per month.[8]

The First Online Culture

After the messages for the day were sent, many telegraph operators used their free time to chat with other operators across the country. Telegraph operators who communicated with each other on a regular basis often became friends. Many were able to identify other operators they knew by the way they sent code.

Experienced telegraph operators were able to tell the slight difference in the pattern of dots and dashes even before the person on the other end sent his or her identity.

Chats over the telegraph line could be about anything. Gossip, weather, music, events in the news, and many other topics gave operators something to discuss when no messages needed to be relayed over the wire. In an article for *McClure's* magazine in 1902, "Telegraph Talk and Talkers," L. C. Hall wrote:

> Stories are told, opinions exchanged, and laughs enjoyed, just as if the participants were sitting together at a club. They grow to know each other's habits, moods, and foibles, their likes and dislikes and when there is a break in the circle through the death of a member, his absence is felt just as in personal association.[9]

Woman telegraph operators often worked in separate areas from men. But that did not keep the male and female operators from communicating over the telegraph lines. Sometimes, chats on the telegraph line between men and women led to romance, and even marriage proposals.

All this could be compared with people today who use computers to e-mail or send instant messages to friends over the Internet.

But after awhile, some company bosses demanded the practice of chatting over telegraph lines be stopped. They felt it was too distracting and took their employees' time away from the business of sending telegrams. The *Circular to the Operators of the New York and Boston Magnetic Telegraph Association*, published in 1848, gave the following warning to the company's employees, "Much useless talk has been indulged among many operators. . . . The operator who is found talking about the weather, Broadway amusements, or like frivolous concerns, over the Line, will have early notice that his services can be dispensed with."[10]

Thomas Edison

Several men who began their career as telegraph operators later became famous. From a young age, Thomas Edison heard stories of brave pioneers who built telegraph lines in the untamed West. He wanted to know everything he possibly could about how it worked. One telegraph stationmaster who had emigrated from Scotland described the telegraph by saying "it was like a long dog with its tail in Scotland and its head in London. When you pull its tail in Edinburgh [Scotland] it barks in London [England]."[11] Edison had increasing interest in the idea of sending messages over wire by means of the invisible energy of electricity.

When Thomas was only eleven years old, he read a science handbook that described in detail how the telegraph system operated. After that, he was determined to set up a crude telegraph line of his own. Late in his life, Edison wrote, "I built a telegraph wire between our houses . . . separated by woods. The wire was that used for suspending stove pipes, the insulators were small bottles pegged on ten-penny nails driven into the trees. It worked fine."[12]

Edison learned the code from a nearby stationmaster and took his first job as a telegraph operator at the Port Huron, Michigan, train station. In the years that followed, he worked sending and receiving messages at telegraph stations across the United States and Canada.

Edison was soon known as one of the best telegraph operators in the country. In 1868, he received a promotion and moved to Boston, Massachusetts, to take a job as a telegraph operator for Western Union. Even then, Edison knew he wanted to be an inventor. While he was employed by Western Union, Edison worked on several inventions in his spare time—

including a vote counter and stock ticker. (A stock ticker was a special telegraph designed for use by financial markets and investors.)

When he was twenty-one years old, Edison decided to give up his job at Western Union so

Thomas Edison began his career as a telegraph operator and later became one of America's most famous inventors.

he could devote more time to his inventions. His first invention after leaving the company was a duplex telegraph, a system that could send and receive messages at the same time. He borrowed eight hundred dollars so he could set up a demonstration between New York City and Rochester, New York. However, the operator in New York City did not understand Edison's directions, so the demonstration failed.

Edison was broke. He borrowed enough for a trip to New York City. When he arrived, he was fortunate enough to be at the Gold Indicator Company when their stock ticker broke. Edison knew how to repair it, and was hired at three hundred dollars a month—a large salary at the time.

Edison sometimes worked up to twenty hours a day. A famous saying of his was: "Genius is one percent inspiration and 99 percent perspiration." During his lifetime, Edison was granted a patent for 1,093 inventions. This earned him the nickname "The Wizard of Menlo Park." (Menlo Park was the address of the New Jersey laboratory where Edison worked on his inventions at the time.)

In 1874, Edison invented a quadruplex telegraph system. This allowed two messages to be sent in opposite directions at the same time. Western Union paid Edison forty thousand dollars for the invention. This was a lot of money at the time.

A year later, Emile Baudot, an engineer with the French Telegraph Service, invented a printing telegraph that six operators at a time could use. The

In his various laboratories, Thomas Edison worked on many experiments. This laboratory was in Building 2 of his facility in West Orange, New Jersey. He moved to the town in 1888.

Baudot telegraph machine sent 180 letters or numbers per minute. It was used by telegraph offices throughout the world for seventy years before it became obsolete.

Baudot's invention improved upon Edison's groundbreaking achievements. However, Edison was not the only telegraph operator that went on to greater things.

Andrew Carnegie

Andrew Carnegie, who would go on to gain his wealth in the steel business, once worked as a telegraph

Andrew Carnegie started working in a telegraph office at the age of fourteen and went on to gain wealth in the steel business.

operator. Starting in 1849, at the age of fourteen, Carnegie worked as a messenger boy in a Pittsburgh, Pennsylvania, telegraph office. His salary was $2.50 per week. Even though he did not earn much money, Carnegie used the opportunity to improve himself. Not long after he started work, Carnegie memorized the faces, names, and addresses when he made deliveries. That made it possible for him to save time. Sometimes, he recognized people on the street and delivered their telegrams right there.

Within a month of taking the job, Carnegie asked his supervisor, Mr. Reid, to teach him Morse code.

The boss was so impressed with Carnegie's skills that he promoted him to the position of telegraph operator. His salary was raised to twenty dollars a month. Carnegie later said:

> My entrance into the telegraph office was a transition from darkness to light—from firing a small engine in

a dark and dirty cellar into a clean office with bright windows and a literary atmosphere, with books, newspapers, pens, and pencils all around me. I was the happiest boy alive.[13]

At that time, telegraph messages were routinely printed on a narrow strip of tape. The only sound telegraph operators could hear was a light clicking sound as the machines' metal relays opened and closed. When Carnegie was working at the telegraph office, he learned to read Morse code by listening to the clicks. It took many hours of practice for Carnegie to learn the code. He also needed to interpret the spacing that determined whether the person on the other end was transmitting a dot or dash. At the time Carnegie taught himself to do this, only two other telegraph operators in the United States were known to be able to read Morse code messages by sound alone.

In 1853, Carnegie decided to accept a job as the personal telegrapher and assistant to the superintendent of the Pennsylvania Railroad's western division, Thomas Scott. Carnegie's pay was thirty-five dollars per month. While he was working for Scott, Carnegie learned all about the railroad industry. Before long, he started coming to his boss with ideas that could improve the business. Carnegie suggested the railroad keep the telegraph office open twenty-four hours a day in case of emergency. He also suggested that the railroad burn railroad cars that were derailed in an accident. That would clear the railroad tracks much quicker so other trains could pass without delay.

During the Civil War, both Union and Confederate soldiers tried to cut the enemy's telegraph lines. This soldier is cutting the lines in such a way that the cut can not be seen by the enemy.

In May 1861, after the Civil War had begun, Scott was appointed as assistant secretary of war. He was put in charge of military railroads and telegraphs. By then, Carnegie had worked his way up to superintendent of the Western Division. He did not want to leave his position and move to Washington. But Scott told Carnegie the job in Washington was very important to the nation.

When Carnegie arrived in Washington, he became the supervisor of United States government telegraph communications. During the Civil War, the South was doing everything possible to disrupt the North's communications. One time, Carnegie had to travel by train to Annapolis, Maryland, to restore communications. While the train passed Elbridge Junction, Carnegie saw where some telegraph wires had been pulled down by Confederate troops. Carnegie ordered the train to stop and got out to cut the wires loose. One wire hit him in the face, causing a scar he would have all his life.

Growth of the Telegraph System

Big businesses were the primary customers of the telegraph. Telegrams were expensive, and individuals usually sent a telegram only for emergencies. Railroads were also a major user of the telegraph. The telegraph helped connect people in the western territories to the rest of the nation.

Except for the money Congress granted Morse to build the first experimental line from Washington, D.C., to Baltimore, Maryland, telegraph line construction in the United States was funded by investors who believed enough in the electric telegraph system to back it with their own money. Still, the web of telegraph lines grew quickly across the United States.

In 1846, a New York newspaper writer boasted, "While England by her government has got with great labor 175 miles [actually 200] of telegraph into operation . . . the United States with her individual enterprise has now in successful operation 1,269 miles. This is American enterprise."[14]

Within a decade after the first American telegraph line went into operation, twenty-three thousand miles of wire crisscrossed the United States. The invention of the telegraph and the wise investments of people that realized its value made the rapid communications people had long dreamed of a reality.

During the mid-to-late 1800s, Western Union became one of the largest telegraph services in America. The company originally went into business as the New York and Mississippi Valley Printing Telegraph Company. It started buying up small telegraph companies around the nation until the company controlled the largest network of telegraph lines in the United States.

The telegraph was very important in the development of the West. Once telegraph lines to the West were in operation, railroad travel was safer and businessmen could get the information they needed to compete with companies in the more populated areas of the nation.

The telegraph was also very useful to the United States government. With the growing tension between the North and South during the first half of the nineteenth century, government and military leaders with access to a telegraph line had an advantage. When the Civil War was underway, telegraph operators played an important role in relaying government communication. In 1860, approximately two thousand men were employed as telegraphers. At the time, over half of all telegraphers employed were members of the Union Army's Military Telegraph Corps.

The rapid communication made possible by the telegraph had its own set of problems. Because of the telegraph's speed and the number of telegraph operators that knew the contents of messages before they arrived, other new issues also had to be addressed. These issues included confidentiality, fraud, and privacy rights. Security of government messages being sent by means of the telegraph was also a big concern, especially during the Civil War.

In 1861, Western Union decided to construct a telegraph line between St. Joseph, Missouri, and Sacramento, California. For the first time, the Transcontinental Telegraph allowed people living in the West to have rapid communication with the East Coast. The line was used until the transcontinental railroad was completed in 1869 and the telegraph lines were moved to follow its route.

This drawing shows soldiers putting up a telegraph wire during the Civil War. The telegraph system was a useful method of communication during this conflict.

When telegraph lines reached into California in 1861, they caused the Pony Express to go out of business. Until that time, the Pony Express, with its relay of swift horseback riders, was the fastest way to get a message to the West. The Pony Express ran for almost two thousand miles, from St. Joseph, Missouri, to Sacramento, California. But once coast-to-coast telegraph service was available, there was no longer a need for the Pony Express. When the service ended, the *Sacramento Bee* published this tribute: "Farewell, Pony: Farewell and forever. . . . Rest upon your honors; be satisfied with them, your destiny has been fulfilled—a

NOTICE.

BY ORDERS FROM THE EAST,

THE PONY EXPRESS

WILL be DISCONTINUED.

The Last Pony coming this way left Atchinson, Kansas, yesterday.

oc25-1t WELLS, FARGO & CO., Agents.

This poster announced that the Pony Express was going out of business. With the completion of the Transcontinental Telegraph, the Pony Express was no longer the fastest method of relaying messages from the East Coast to the West.

new and higher power [the telegraph] has superseded you."[15]

By 1863, many telegraph operators were overworked by business, personal, and military messages due to the Civil War. So they formed the National Telegraphic Union to protect their rights. The union admitted both men and women and paid benefits to telegraph operators who were out of work or retired.

The telegraph was a great benefit to newspaper editors. Once they had access to the telegraph, they could report events that happened thousands of miles away as quickly as they reported local happenings. News that once took days or weeks to arrive by horse, train, or steamship, was now as close as the nearest telegraph office.

The stock market was also affected by the telegraph. When the New York Stock Exchange put the electric stock ticker into use in 1867, people in distant parts of the country could buy stocks without having to wait for their orders to arrive through the postal system.

But just like anyone else, telegraph operators sometimes made mistakes. Humorists of the time made jokes about these problems, just as comedians today often make jokes about the problems of the Postal Service—like lost and late mail.

Underwater Telegraph Cables

Even with all the improvements in communication the telegraph provided, Morse believed that his invention could do more. The telegraph, Morse felt, could be used not only to communicate across dry ground, but across the ocean as well. He once said, "If it can go ten miles without stopping, I can make it go around the world."[16]

In 1845, Morse laid the first telegraph cables to cross the Hudson River and New York Harbor. It was a good plan, but the only materials Morse had to insulate the wires were asphalt, wax, and shellac. And that was not enough to keep the water from penetrating the cable. Once water touched the wires inside the cables, no communication over the lines was possible.

Morse did not know it, but even before he laid the lines, the answer to his problem had already been discovered. A new type of rubber called "gutta-percha" was first developed in 1843. By 1847, it was routinely being used on underwater telegraph cables.

The Transatlantic Telegraph

Morse hoped to lay a telegraph cable across the Atlantic Ocean. Many members of Congress ridiculed him when he asked them to help finance the project. However, several important scientists, including Michael Faraday, believed that Morse's idea was workable. But other scientists, including French physicist Jacques Babinet, believed it was impossible to lay an insulated telegraph cable under the ocean and expect it to work.

In 1854, Cyrus W. Field, a wealthy scientist and New York paper merchant, decided to lay an underwater telegraph cable from the United States to England. He convinced a number of wealthy men in New York to help him finance the venture. The business was named the New York, Newfoundland, and London Telegraph Company.

In 1856, Field's company finished laying the first section of the transatlantic telegraph between New York and St. John's, Newfoundland. Field then traveled to England to find more investors for the project. With their money, he formed the Atlantic Telegraph Company in London. Their job was to lay insulated telegraph cable across the ocean from England to Newfoundland, Canada.

Two attempts to lay a transatlantic cable in 1857 failed. But the company's third attempt on August 7, 1858, was successful. For the first time ever, the transatlantic telegraph line allowed people in the United States and Europe to communicate with minimal delay.

Although there were some problems with the telegraph line, people on both sides of the ocean were thrilled. Morse code messages were received across the ocean shortly after they were transmitted. This marked the beginning of a new era in electric communications.

But on September 1, about four weeks after the underwater transatlantic cable had first been installed, the insulation cracked and allowed water to seep into the cable. After that, no one could communicate over the line.

After this failure, it was difficult for anyone to raise money to build another transatlantic cable. The United States government became involved with the Civil War and did not want to pay for another attempt. But the British government put together a group of scientists to investigate the possibility. The scientists studied the idea of a transatlantic cable for almost two years. They tried all sorts of experiments to see what insulating materials would be most likely to last underwater. When they were finished, they were certain that laying a successful transatlantic cable was possible.

With the research of many well-known scientists to back him up, Field was willing to try once more. He got together his investors and on July 15, 1865, the project was ready to begin. In England, the cable that would bridge the Atlantic was hauled onto a huge ocean-going ship called *The Great Eastern*. During the first week the crew laid out over twelve hundred miles of cable. Everyone on board was thrilled with the progress they had made.

But when they had only about 550 miles to go, the cable snapped and fell to the bottom of the ocean. The crew tried frantically to raise the cable, but nothing worked. However, on March 31, 1866, they were ready to try again. It took five months from the time new cable was made until it was laid across the ocean. It was then ready to transmit the first message across the Atlantic Ocean. At last, there was a working telegraph cable between England and the United States. At last, the idea that Morse had supported for so many years had come true.

News of the Transcontinental Railroad

On May 10, 1869, the tracks of the Central Pacific and the Union Pacific Railway were connected at Promontory, Utah, to form the transcontinental railroad. This was the first time a train could travel directly from New York City to California. This was a very important step in connecting the West to the rest of the nation.

In 1869, the transcontinental railroad was completed in Promontory, Utah. A telegraph signal was sent as the final railroad spike was pounded in to the ground. In the center of this drawing, a man is about to hit the spike.

A special telegraph wire was attached to the final railroad spike. When the spike was pounded in to the ground, it would send a signal to telegraph operators along the line. When the president of the Pacific Railway tried to hit the final spike, he missed. To avoid embarrassment for the railway, the telegraph operator sent a fake spike signal, and the word DONE.

Historian Stephen Ambrose wrote:

> Together, the transcontinental railroad and the telegraph made modern America possible. Things that could not be imagined before the Civil War now became common. A nationwide stock market, for example. A continent-wide economy in which people, agricultural products, coal and minerals moved wherever someone wanted to send them and did so cheaply and quickly. A continent-wide culture in which mail and popular magazines and books that used to cost dollars per ounce and had taken forever to get from the East to the West Coast, now cost pennies and got there in a few days.[17]

The Telegraph Makes Morse Rich

By the 1860s, profits from the telegraph had made Morse a wealthy man. He could now use his time and money to do anything he liked. Morse was appointed as a vice president of the new Metropolitan Museum of Art. He was also a trustee of Vassar College. Morse donated some of his money to Yale University and other organizations.

In 1871, while Morse was still living, the telegraph industry honored him by building a bronze statue of him in Central Park in New York City. It showed him sitting beside a telegraph instrument, holding a piece of paper that said "What hath God wrought" in dots and dashes.

While Morse was not the only person to invent a telegraph, the effort he made to promote his version of the electric telegraph system helped to speed its development. The communications of individuals, governments, and business quickly improved because of Morse's invention. He died in 1872, only a few years before Alexander Graham Bell invented the telephone.

5

THE TELEPHONE ENTERS AMERICAN LIFE

While the telegraph gave Americans faster communication than had ever been possible, it was not the same as being able to talk to someone directly. Messages had to go through an operator to be translated into dots and dashes. Then, an operator on the other end had to translate a message for the person that would receive it. Then, a messenger had to be sent to deliver it.

Because of this drawback, some farsighted inventors attempted to discover a method where voice could be transmitted by means of electricity. This would make back-and-forth communication over distances a lot quicker.

In 1860, Johann Philip Reis, a German schoolteacher, invented a machine that could transmit sounds through a wire. In 1861, Reis gave his first public demonstration. When he sang through the device, some people in a building about three hundred feet away were able to recognize the tune. But his machine

The telegraph system relied on a system of operators and messengers. Here, a group of message boys await orders to deliver a telegraph in Indianapolis, Indiana.

did not have good sound quality, and he did not try to patent it. To Reis, this was more of a curiosity than a practical invention.

Bell and Gray Race Against Each Other

In the 1870s, Alexander Graham Bell was working hard on his idea for a telephone. But he heard that another inventor, Elisha Gray, who was born in Barnesville, Ohio, was also working on a device that could transmit voice over a wire. While Bell had a background in teaching speech, Gray had the advantage of a good education in the study of electricity.

While Gray was attending Oberlin College, he learned about electricity and was fascinated by the science. In 1867, Gray had received a patent for an improved version of the telegraph relay.

Bell was worried that Gray would be able to invent a telephone before he did. The first person who succeeded in developing the invention and acquiring a patent would gain all the honor and profits.

Bell knew that he needed all the help he could get to reach his goal. In March 1875, he traveled to Washington to meet with Joseph Henry. Henry had developed an early version of the telegraph and had also built a huge electromagnet.

Bell told Henry what he had accomplished with both the harmonic telegraph and telephone. After reviewing Bell's inventions, Henry encouraged Bell to set aside everything else and concentrate on developing a working model of the telephone. Bell was concerned that he did not know enough about electricity. But Henry encouraged him to learn more about it so he could complete the project.

When Bell returned home, he dismissed nearly all his deaf students. This cut Bell's income, but it gave him more time to work on his inventions. Bell had to borrow money from Thomas Watson to continue his work, but he was certain his idea for a telephone would succeed.

As close as Bell was to achieving his goals, problems arose that kept him from making the discoveries necessary to complete his inventions. In June 1875,

Bell wrote a letter to his parents. He said, "I am like a man in a fog. . . . I know I am close to the land for which I am bound and when the fog lifts I shall see it right before me."[1]

While Bell did not know as much about electricity as some inventors, he did have one advantage. His work as a speech teacher gave him an excellent background in sound and how it is produced. This helped him understand how to design a device that allowed human speech to be transmitted by electricity.

Once Bell discovered how to transmit sound through a wire, he repeated the experiment several times to confirm what was happening. Then, he drew a design for a primitive telephone transmitter and receiver and asked Watson to build it for him.

When they first tested it, Bell was not able to hear anything. But Watson, who had better hearing than Bell, was certain he could make out a word now and then. At this point, Bell was well on his way to inventing a telephone. But he had much work to do before it was ready to market and demonstrate to the public.

Bell realized that other scientists and inventors were also working to find a way to transmit the human voice over wire. He hoped that he could find the answer to the problem before they did.

On February 14, 1876, Gray filed a "caveat," an announcement of the invention he soon hoped to patent with the United States Patent Office. When he filed this document, he thought he had won the race. He had no way of knowing that only two hours earlier,

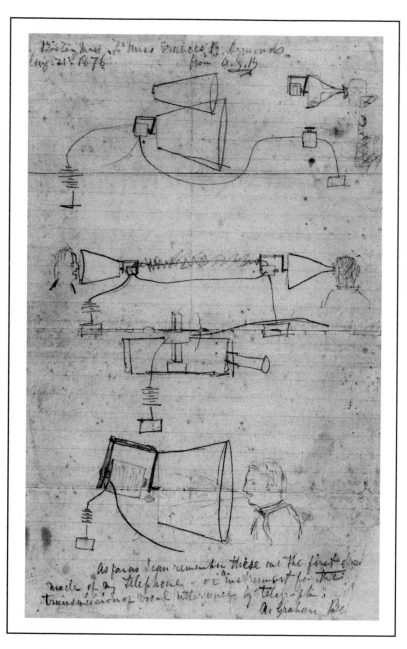

While working toward the invention of the telephone, Alexander Graham Bell sketched primitive images of the device, like this early drawing.

one of Bell's investors, Gardiner Hubbard, had filed Bell's application for an actual patent on a similar device at the same patent office in Washington, D.C. At the time these papers were filed, both inventions were in the experimental stage. Neither Bell's nor Gray's idea for a telephone was developed enough to put into operation.

For years, Bell and Gray would fight in court over who should be named the inventor of the telephone. While Gray's application to the patent office was a few hours later than Bell's, Gray felt the idea he submitted was more accurate and complete. But every time a judgment was handed down, Bell won. The case was finally settled out of court in Bell's favor in 1879.

Still, Gray found ways to profit from the telephone business. During his lifetime, Gray was granted nearly seventy patents. One of his patents was for the telautograph, a device that could transmit handwriting and drawings over the telephone line. This was an early form of today's fax machine.

Bell Demonstrates the Telephone

Bell went to work promoting the telephone to a wider audience. He gave public demonstrations to scientists in the Boston area. Some people were impressed, but few really understood Bell's invention or had any idea of the important role it could play in communication.

Gardiner Hubbard heard that a huge exhibition was being planned in Philadelphia, Pennsylvania, to celebrate the United States' one hundredth anniversary.

He then encouraged Bell to obtain a space there to demonstrate the telephone. If the telephone was put on exhibit at the Centennial Exhibition, Hubbard knew that important people from all over the world would see it.

Bell agreed. Even though many other inventors would have their work on display at the Centennial Exhibition, this was his best opportunity to gain much-needed publicity. Government leaders, wealthy businessmen, and scientists from all over the world were certain to attend. Those were exactly the people he needed to see a demonstration of his telephone.

On June 25, 1876, the Emperor of Brazil, Pedro II, came to the Centennial Exhibition. Emperor Pedro had visited Bell earlier and wanted to know more about his work. Bell went to the end of the hall and began talking over the phone's transmitter. Emperor Pedro was holding the receiver at the other end of the exhibition area. Suddenly he was able to hear what Bell was saying!

After that, word spread quickly about the telephone. Many government leaders, scientists, inventors, and other important people at the exhibition wanted to learn more about the telephone and see how it worked.

Bell also demonstrated the telephone in Britain. Queen Victoria was very impressed by Bell's invention. After learning about the telephone, she wrote in her journal, "A Professor Bell explained the whole process which is the most extraordinary."[2]

SIR WILLIAM EXPRESSED GREAT INTEREST IN MY INVENTION AND SAID THAT HE WISHED TO HAVE A GLIMPSE OF THE INSTRUMENTS BEFORE HE LEFT THE BUILDING . . .

IT WAS REALLY A PLEASURE TO SEE HIM EXAMINING THE APPARATUS. HE WAS SO ABSORBED AND EXCITED HE FORGOT ALL ABOUT POOR ME . . .

AT LAST HE LOOKED UP AND SAW ME—AND APOLOGIZED FOR HAVING KEPT ME WAITING SO LONG . . . HE STATED THAT HE WAS COMING TO THE BUILDING ON SUNDAY WITH THE EMPEROR DON PEDRO—TO SEE MR. GRAY'S INSTRUMENTS AND ASKED ME TO EXHIBIT MINE AT THE SAME TIME!

I MUST SAY I DON'T LIKE THIS AT ALL—AND WOULD RATHER AVOID A DIRECT COLLISION WITH MR. GRAY IF POSSIBLE.[3]

In a letter to his future wife, Mabel Hubbard, Bell expresses his nervousness at having to demonstrate his instruments to Emperor Don Pedro at the same time as Elisha Gray. Bell and Gray were often locked in legal battles over rights to the telephone.

Encouraged by Queen Victoria's response, Bell tried to promote the telephone in England. In one letter to English businessmen he wrote,

> At the present time we have a perfect network of gas-pipes and water-pipes throughout our large cities. . . . In a similar manner, it is conceivable that cables of telephone wires would be laid underground, or suspended overhead, communicating by branch wires with private dwellings, country houses, shops, manufacturers, etc. . . . establishing direct communication between any two places in the city. Such a plan as this . . . [will] be the outcome of the introduction of the telephone to the public. . . . I believe in the future, wires will unite the head offices of the Telephone Company in different cities, and a man in one part of the country may communicate by word of mouth with another in a distant place.[4]

The Telephone Business in the United States

Bell was certain that the telephone would eventually be a success in America. Once he could prove his invention to the American public, Bell felt that everyone in the country would want to own a telephone. In time, Bell believed that the general public would view having a telephone in their home or place of business as a necessity.

In November 1876, Bell wrote a letter to his fiancée saying, "When people can order everything they want from the store without leaving home and chat comfortably with each other . . . over some piece of gossip, every person will desire to put money in our pockets by having telephones."[5]

In April 1877, the first permanent experimental telephone line was installed in Boston. The line relayed calls between Charles Williams' electrical shop on Court Street and his home, about three miles away. In May, a Boston area banker who wanted to make calls between his office and his home ordered the first commercial telephone line.

Bell investor Gardiner Hubbard decided to run an ad for telephone service. While Bell's early telephone models did not sound nearly as good as telephones do today, they were the first devices that made it possible to communicate by voice over moderate distances. The advertisement read:

> [c]onversation can easily be carried on after slight practice and with occasional repetition of a word or sentence. On first listening to the Telephone, though the sound is perfectly audible, the articulation seems to be indistinct; but after a few trials the ear becomes accustomed to the peculiar sound.[6]

To help promote the invention, Bell and Watson demonstrated the telephone to audiences throughout the Northeast. They took a phone on stage and had receivers throughout the hall where people could listen. But the idea of speech being transmitted through an electric wire was so new that some people were frightened. A reporter for the *New York Herald* said the telephone was "almost supernatural."[7]

In April 1877, Bell and Watson used the telephone to transmit a conversation between Boston and New York over railroad telegraph lines. This was their first public test of long-distance communication by telephone. Their equipment was able to relay the message over the wire, but the sound quality was very poor by today's standards.

In July 1877, Gardiner Hubbard formed the Bell Telephone Company. Watson supervised the shop where telephones were built. So the Charles Williams shop was in effect the first research and development lab of the Bell Telephone Company. Once Bell saw that the company was a success, he wanted to get away from the business world for a while. So, he left for England after he got married.

The first telephone lines that Bell's company built could only connect telephones between one home or business and another home or business. Before the telephone was to be a more useful means of communication, a new system had to be devised. Telephone subscribers needed to speak to more than one location without being directly connected to them. The telephone exchange, where calls could be connected between any two subscribers in the system, was the next important step in the expansion of the telephone communications network.

The First Telephone Exchange

The telephone switchboard was introduced in 1878. This new invention allowed operators to connect subscribers' phones through a single telephone exchange system. To place a call through this system, subscribers called the operator and asked to be connected with the person with whom they wanted to speak. With the new invention, any subscriber could talk to any other subscriber.

The first commercial telephone exchange switchboard was put into service in New Haven, Connecticut, on January 28, 1878. Twenty-one businesses subscribed to the service. Teenage boys were hired as the first telephone switchboard operators. At the time, telephone numbers had not yet been assigned. Only the name of the subscriber was used to find the right connections.

The famous humorist and writer, Mark Twain, was living in Hartford, Connecticut, at the time. He did not let the occasion pass without a joke. Twain said, "If Bell had invented a muffler or gag, he would have done a real service. Here we have been hollering 'Shut up' to our neighbors for centuries, and now you fellows come along and seek to complicate matters."[8] Three days after the first switchboard began to operate, another telephone exchange went into business in Meriden, Connecticut.

Once the switchboard exchange system was proven to work, telephone exchange systems were built across the country. In 1879, the Lowell, Massachusetts, telephone system became the first to use telephone numbers instead of names.

Telephone exchange offices continued to hire teenage boys as operators to connect the calls. Every time a call came in, the boys had to find out who the caller wanted to speak with, then run all over the exchange office to find the right place to plug in the wires. Some boys did a good job and took their responsibilities as a telephone operator seriously. But others were impatient and rude to the customers. As a result, by the early 1900s telephone exchanges hired mostly women as operators.[9]

Telephone operators connected calls through an exchange switchboard. In 1941, these operators put in a day's work in Aberdeen, Maryland.

The early telephone models, like the one shown here, served as both a transmitter and receiver.

The earliest telephones used by the American public were built inside a metal box. The box served as both a transmitter and receiver. In the next step of the telephone's development, the telephone box was built so it could hang on the wall. The receiver and transmitter, two separate devices, were attached by wire and hung down from the main telephone box.

By the early 1900s, most telephones were built into wooden boxes that hung on the wall. They had a receiver, a mouthpiece, and a crank. When a telephone subscriber wanted to make a call, he or she picked up the receiver and turned the crank. The operator then came online and said, "Number, please?"[10] Moments later, the caller could speak with any subscriber in the telephone system.

In 1900, the price of having a telephone installed was $12.50 per month. Long-distance calls cost extra. At the time, the average American wage was only $38.50 a month. Because of the high cost, most telephone customers in the United States at that time were businesses or rich people.[11]

Improvements in Long-Distance Service

Even though the early model telephone worked fairly well over short distances, it was difficult to hear voices over long telephone lines. If long-distance telephone service was to be a success, there had to be a way to strengthen the signal over long distances. This was one of Bell's big challenges.

THE WESTERN UNION TELEGRAPH COMPANY . . . AGREES TO WITHDRAW FROM THE TELEPHONE BUSINESS IN THE UNITED STATES, LEAVING THE FIELD ENTIRELY CLEAR TO THE COMPANY OPERATING UNDER THE BELL PATENTS. ALL PERSONS WHO HOLD RIGHTS FROM OTHER COMPANIES WILL BE LICENSED UNDER THESE PATENTS. THE WESTERN UNION FURTHER AGREES TO ALLOW THE BELL TELEPHONE COMPANY A PERCENTAGE ON THE TELEGRAPHIC BUSINESS RECEIVED THROUGH ITS INSTRUMENTS, AND TO COOPERATE TO THE EXTENT OF ITS POWER.

UNDER THIS ADJUSTMENT THE BELL TELEPHONE COMPANY ACQUIRES ALL THE TELEPHONIC INVENTIONS OF ELISHA GRAY OF CHICAGO, OF THOMAS EDISON, OF GEORGE PHELPS, AND ALL OTHERS WHO HAD ASSIGNED THEIR INTERESTS TO THE WESTERN UNION OR OTHER ALLIED COMPANIES. . . .

THE SUM PAID BY THE BELL COMPANY TO SECURE THIS MOST SATISFACTORY SETTLEMENT IS NOT STATED, BUT IS PRESUMED TO BE A LARGE ONE . . . BELL TELEPHONE HAS A FUTURE OF FAME AND FORTUNE IN STORE FOR IT NOT SURPASSED BY ANY OF THE GREAT DISCOVERIES OF OUR TIME.[12]

This October 25, 1879 article in the Boston Daily Advertiser *predicts the success of the Bell Telephone company after its settlement with Western Union Telegraph Company.*

In the late 1800s, experimental telephone lines between large cities—including New York, Philadelphia, and Chicago—were in place. But even under the best conditions, communication by telephone at distances over one thousand miles was nearly impossible.

But in 1900, Michael Pupin, a professor at Columbia University, came up with a solution. He found a way to electrically load a line so less power would be lost. His invention made possible the first long-distance line from New York City to Denver, Colorado, in 1911.[13]

The Rise of Telephone Companies

On March 3, 1885, American Bell, the company founded by Alexander Graham Bell, decided to create the American Telephone and Telegraph Company. The company was put in charge of building and operating the growing long-distance telephone network.

Construction of the American Telephone and Telegraph (AT&T) network's long-distance system was started in New York. They had built telephone lines as far as Chicago in 1892.

Until 1894, only Bell Telephone and those companies it sold permission to were permitted to operate telephone systems in the United States. That year, Bell's second patent expired. After that, the business was open to anyone. Over the next twenty years, more than six thousand independent telephone companies went into business. During that time the number of telephones Americans owned grew from 285,000 to

3.3 million. Companies also started to serve many areas that had never had telephone service before. However, many of the companies still had no way to connect subscribers from one company's system to another.[14]

While some telephone companies used slightly different systems, they all had one thing in common. Every call had to be connected by an operator, who had to stand at switchboards and manually plug in the correct wires to make each call.

Job Openings for Women

When Emma Nutt went to work for Edwin Holmes and his Telephone Dispatch Company in Boston, Massachusetts, in 1878, she became the first woman telephone operator. Before that, she worked as a telegraph operator. Emma Nutt would work thirty-three years as a telephone operator before retiring.

Nearly all telephone operators were women by 1900. At that time, women who wanted a job outside of their home did not have many options. Usually, they had to choose between working as a nurse, teacher, salesclerk, factory worker, or servant.

Many telephone companies were selective about the women they hired. Usually, they had to be unmarried and between the ages of seventeen and twenty-six. The company where Emma Nutt worked refused to hire married women until 1942. To qualify for a job as an operator, a woman had to be tall enough to easily reach the switching equipment. She also had to dress

In addition to connecting calls through a switchboard, early telephone operators were expected to give out information and answer questions.

and wear her hair like a proper middle-class lady of the time. In many areas, Jewish and African-American women were discriminated against and had a very difficult time finding work as telephone operators.

In the early 1900s, women were nearly always paid less than men. Most telephone operators were paid from seven to ten dollars per week. Even then, this would be considered a low wage for a man, but was typical of what women could expect to earn.

Life as an Operator

An operator often had to work from nine to eleven hours a day, six days a week. Telephone operators sometimes had to work on holidays and at nights. When an operator got married, she was usually forced to quit her job at the phone company.

During the early decades of the telephone industry, operators were vital to the system's operation. They were put in charge of switchboards that connected up to two hundred phone lines.

Besides connecting telephone calls, early telephone operators were often expected to give out all sorts of information. Customers often picked up their phones to ask the operator about train schedules, storms, news, and other happenings.

As the telephone industry gained more customers, the demands placed on operators increased. Telephone operators who worked in big city offices were nearly always busy. City operators were sometimes called on to connect several hundred calls an hour. Sometimes, the customers were rude. An article published in an 1898 issue of the *Financial Times* read:

> [Telephone subscribers] employ the call-wire for abusing the operators, frequently using very violent and brutal language to them, so much so that at times they drive them into hysterics. No one can condone the use of violent and abusive language to young ladies, even if they be telephone girls.[15]

To make sure there were no unnecessary delays, telephone company owners hired management teams. These teams created a set of rules that every operator working for the company had to obey. These rules

In this photograph, female telephone operators are shown working at their switchboard. A supervisor stands behind them, making sure everything runs smoothly.

covered everything from how long an operator should spend with a customer to how she should sit. It was against the rules for city operators to chat with customers. Many telephone companies required operators to ask permission if they needed to get a drink or go to the bathroom. If a supervisor caught an operator violating any of these rules, she could be punished or even fired.

The headset and other equipment an operator had to wear to connect calls weighed about six pounds. Operators were required to always sit up straight in their chairs. They were not permitted to cross their legs, or even blow their noses without a supervisor's permission.

Even with all these restrictions, work as a telephone operator gave women who wanted to work outside the home new opportunities. By 1900, the telephone companies were the largest private employer of women.[16]

Telephone operators who worked in rural areas and small towns had much easier lives. They had more freedom and a much lighter schedule. Some rural telephone operators were able to work in their homes. They had a switchboard with the names of every customer on the exchange. Rural telephone operators often wore headsets with long cords so they could finish their household chores while they waited to handle the next call.

A Telephone in the White House

James Garfield had the honor of being the first American president to rent a telephone. In 1878, when Garfield was still a congressman, it was placed on exhibit in his home. Presidents Grover Cleveland and Benjamin Harrison owned telephones, but neither used it very often.

But when President William McKinley came into office, he saw the telephone in a new light. He saw the telephone as a necessity, as well as a convenience. In 1895, McKinley used the telephone in his Canton, Ohio, home to listen to people cheering at the Chicago political convention. He used the telephone in his campaign to run for president and talked over the phone to his campaign managers in thirty-eight states.

Historian Herbert N. Casson wrote that McKinley "came to regard the telephone with a higher degree of appreciation than any of his predecessors had done, and eulogized it on many public occasions. 'It is bringing us all closer together,' was his favorite phrase."[17]

Herbert Hoover (1929–1933) was the first president to actually have a phone on his desk. Presidents before him kept the telephone they used in another area of the White House.

The End of Bell's Life

For the most part, Bell wanted other people to take care of the business end of the telephone system. He preferred to work on his inventions. Throughout his life, Bell enjoyed trying out new ideas to see if they

The invention of the telephone slowly became a vital tool for American presidents during their terms. Here, President William Howard Taft (1857–1930) poses with his hand on a telephone.

would work. Around 1880, Bell invented a device that could transmit sound over a beam of light. While it was never put to practical use, the idea fascinated many scientists. Bell was also interested in aviation and realized that flight would one day play an important role in transportation.

Bell always had an interest in helping deaf people communicate more effectively. For several years, he was president of Clarke School for the Deaf in Northhampton, Massachusetts. Bell also founded the American Association to Promote the Teaching of Speech to the Deaf in 1890, and donated $300,000 of his own money to finance it.

AMERICA GETS CONNECTED

B_y March of 1880, 138 telephone companies with a total of 30,000 customers were doing business in the United States. All were under Bell's license. Seven years later, one hundred fifty thousand people in the United States owned a telephone. Still, only well-to-do families and businesses could afford the luxury of having a telephone. They were far too expensive for the average family. During the 1880s, having a phone installed cost as much as a low-income person could earn in a year.

But even the wealthy sometimes had problems communicating with each other by means of this new invention. After Bell's patent expired in 1894, many different telephone companies existed, often several within a large city. Because these competing telephone businesses often refused to cooperate, it could be difficult to connect with people who subscribed to a different telephone service. To solve this problem, some businesspeople subscribed to more than one telephone service. Gradually, this problem was completely

This man is using an early model telephone. Initially, only well-to-do individuals could afford the luxury of having their own telephones.

solved when AT&T came to control much of the phone service in the United States.

Building Telephone Lines Across the Nation

As with the telegraph, it was challenging and expensive to set telephone poles and string wire through the West. Companies that built the transcontinental telegraph line project received money from the United States government. But the telephone companies did not. So telephone lines were only built if they had promise of making a profit for their investors. Besides, no one knew if the equipment of the time could carry voice signals over such long wires.

Even if a transcontinental telephone line was built, investors knew it would be difficult to keep in operation. Heavy winter storms were certain to break the lines. And it could be days, if not weeks, before a worker could locate and repair breaks in remote locations.

As the network of telephone lines continued to expand into unpopulated areas of the West, linemen became an important part of the telephone service. The job of a lineman included hiking or riding on horseback along the line in search of breaks. Sometimes several inches of ice accumulated on the lines, causing them to sag or break.

Before a national telephone network could be built, someone had to find a way to keep signals from fading. Loading coils, invented in 1899, made voice signals stronger. This made it possible for the network to extend as far west as Denver. To further strengthen signals, researchers at AT&T invented the first practical electrical amplifiers in 1913.

The transcontinental telephone line was a huge project. It required twenty-five hundred tons of copper wire. To support it, 180,000 telephone poles were needed. To keep the signal clear and loud, telephone calls were amplified with loading coils every eight miles. In addition to that, repeaters powered by huge vacuum tubes, a new invention of the time, were used along the line to make certain the calls were loud enough to hear.

In 1915, the transcontinental telephone line between San Francisco and the East went into service. Bell rarely involved himself with the telephone business by then. But he made a point of attending the ceremony in New York. During the festivities, he spoke to Watson in San Francisco. Bell said, "Mr. Watson, come here, I want you!"[1] This was a repeat of the first sentence Bell had spoken over his first working model of the telephone in 1876.

Watson replied that he would be glad to come, but "it would take a week for me to get to you this time."[2]

Bell died on August 2, 1922. Over the following years, telephone service was improved and new types of telephones were invented.

The ease of making calls also increased. At first, callers had to go through an operator to make a call. But as automatic switchboards came into use, phone numbers were issued. Telephone numbers could be easily dialed, and more people wanted to have a phone in their home or office. Larger numbers of telephones had to be manufactured to fill the growing demand, and the price of telephone service fell. This made the telephone affordable for most working-class people.

The Telegraph Industry Stays Alive

While the telephone industry was growing in the early 1900s, telegrams were still the primary means of sending important messages over long distances.

When the telegraph service was new, the railroad, businesses, and the government were the primary users. Telegrams were rarely sent to private households. In fact, telegrams to a home were usually dreaded because they often brought bad news, such as an announcement of the death of a loved one.

To make the idea of sending telegrams to households more popular, telegraph companies came up with new services. They included singing telegrams and prepared greetings similar to what you might find printed on a Christmas or birthday card. This approach worked, and soon people who could afford to send telegrams used them to greet family members, friends, and sweethearts throughout the year. Christmas and Easter telegrams became so popular that telegraph companies were forced to hire extra people and pay overtime wages to handle them all.

A booklet published in 1928 read:

> The telegram no longer bears the badge of emergency and the sight of a messenger approaching your home need no longer raise feelings of foreboding. There are hundreds of telegrams which bring tidings of joy, congratulation or good will, or convey social messages of infinite variety and there are still other thousands which deal with the myriad phases of business operations.[3]

During the early 1900s, the telegraph system saw many improvements that allowed it to handle more messages. One invention allowed several messages to be sent over a wire at the same time. Also, keyboards that looked similar to a typewriter replaced the hand-operated telegraph keys. When an operator typed a letter onto the keyboard, the machine punched holes in a strip of paper. Another machine translated these holes into electrical dots and dashes that were then transmitted over the telegraph lines.

By then, many telegraph offices, especially those in big cities, used receiving machines to handle the increasing amount of message traffic. Receiving machines picked up the electrical dots and dashes, then translated them into actual letters printed on a long strip of paper. Operators at the telegraph station cut the strips of paper and pasted them onto a message form. They were then hand-delivered to their destination.

While these new machines sped up the process of sending telegrams, they brought an end to the first "online culture" where telegraph operators could have person-to-person contact with each other after the messages were sent.

More Americans Have a Telephone

As the industry grew, telephone company executives realized that home phone service was a great untapped market. Still, it took seventy-five years after the invention of the telephone for it to reach half of American households.

After World War II, many Americans could afford to have a telephone installed in their home. They soon discovered that the telephone was a great way not only to conduct business, but also to chat with friends and neighbors. Some people worried that the convenience of telephones would isolate people and discourage them from visiting friends in person. Decades later, the

SOURCE DOCUMENT

THE SYSTEM WAS FIRST INSTALLED IN ONE OF THE MOST TURBULENT DISTRICTS OF THE CITY, AND AT ONCE INCREASED TREMENDOUSLY THE EFFICIENCY OF THE FORCE, CHIEFLY IN THE WAY OF MAKING A RAPID CONCENTRATION AT ANY TROUBLED POINT. ITS SUCCESS WAS SO RAPID THAT BY 1893 NO FEWER THAN ONE THOUSAND STREET STATIONS HAD BEEN INSTALLED ALL OVER CHICAGO, AND IN ADDITION SEVERAL HUNDRED PRIVATE BOXES HAD BEEN PUT IN, GIVING INSTANT COMMUNICATION, AT ANY HOUR OF DAY OR NIGHT, WITH ALL THE STATIONS OF EVERY PRECINCT. SINCE THAT TIME THE IDEA HAS BEEN CARRIED EVEN FARTHER IN VARIOUS WAYS, NOT ONLY IN CHICAGO, BUT IN OTHER CITIES.[4]

A successful police-force communication system in Chicago is described in a document published by the Government Census Bureau in 1906. The system combined both the telegraph and the telephone.

same worries would be raised about people spending too much time chatting over the Internet.

Telephones in American Homes

When telephones first became available, only the wealthy could afford the service. Often, it was considered the job of a household servant to answer the phone.

Even then, some people had begun to realize that telephones could have wider applications. Executives used home phones mostly for business. But soon, other uses for the phone were found. Once enough telephones were in operation, they were used to order groceries and other goods, socialize, or contact a repairman to help with a household emergency.

During the early 1900s, many people still did not understand the telephone and how it operated. In 1916, AT&T printed a statement called "The Kingdom of the Subscriber" to answer the most commonly-asked questions. It read:

> In the development of the telephone system, the subscriber is the dominant factor. His ever-growing requirements inspire invention, lead to endless scientific research, and make necessary vast improvements and extensions. . . .
>
> The telephone cannot think or talk for you, but it carries your thought where you will. It's yours to use. . . .
>
> The telephone is essentially democratic, it carries the voice of the child and the grown-up with equal speed and directness. . . .

It is not only the implement of the individual, but it fulfills the needs of all the people. . . .[5]

In some areas, the telephone was used as a service to broadcast news, weather, music, and religious services. The telephone was also promoted as a sales tool and a way to call doctors.

As early as the 1900s, some businesses decided to use the telephone as a means of advertising their products and services to telephone customers. An article published in the Rochester, New York, *Union and Advertiser* described how these early telemarketers annoyed one busy woman:

"My telephone is far more of a nuisance to me than it is a convenience," said a housekeeper yesterday, "and I think I will have it removed, if I am called up as much in the future as I have been during the past week by theater agents, and business firms, who abuse the telephone privilege, using it as a means of advertising. . . . These are samples of a telephone annoyance that I would like to be freed from."[6]

As time went on, telephone subscribers discovered that the phone was a wonderful way to speak to friends. It was much easier to make a call instead of getting dressed up and taking a carriage or car ride across town.

People in cities and towns were the first to have telephone service. But when farmers learned about the advantages of having a phone, they wanted telephone service as well. A telephone could provide farmers with information they needed, such as weather reports and market prices. It could be used to call for help in case of an emergency. And having a telephone would make farm life less lonely. But the telephone companies were more interested in stringing wire in urban areas, where it was more profitable. To solve the problem, farmers who were frustrated by the lack of service often had to band together and set up telephone systems for themselves.

Small-Town Telephone Systems

While the East was being connected, people living in the western and rural areas of the United States grew tired of waiting for the telephone network to come into their regions. As with the telegraph, they were often the last to benefit from modern electric communication.

Because of this, some rural areas and small towns set up their own telephone service. These small telephone exchanges were often run out of a home, farm, or small business.

The first telephones to be installed in North Dakota, for example, were put into service on the Bonanza farm in 1876. The telephones they used originally came from Philadelphia. They were battery operated and were used for speedy communications between nearby farms owned by the same family.

The first real telephone exchange in Fargo, North Dakota, the Fargo Moorhead Telephone Exchange, went into operation on June 7, 1881. The system cost five thousand dollars to build. The switchboard that operated the exchange was placed in a local hotel.

Telephone lines helped connect remote communities in the western and rural areas of the United States.

When the exchange went into business, they had only twenty-five subscribers, which included a hotel, horse stable, grocery store, gold mine, and other area businesses.

By the end of June 1881, ten miles of telephone wire connected a hundred subscribers in the Fargo area. In 1881, the cost of having a phone in Fargo was $4.98 a month for a private line, $4.10 per month for a line two telephone customers could use, and $3.51 per month for a line that four customers could use.

People living in rural areas often used party lines—telephone lines where more than one household used the same connection—to listen to gossip. When someone talked on a party line, he or she never knew how many other people on the circuit might be listening.

In 1887, telephone subscribers in Fargo felt like they were connected to the outside world when their system was connected to a phone company in St. Cloud, Minnesota. But until 1939, no one in Fargo could make a call without the help of an operator. On July 11, 1939, direct dial service was established in Fargo. Fargo's history of establishing its own telephone service was typical of an isolated western town.[7]

Telephone Service Continues to Improve

Over the decades, telephone companies have continued to improve and expand their services. Call waiting, three-party calling services, calling cards, and caller ID are now common phrases in the American vocabulary. Microwave, satellite, and fiber-optic connections made it possible for telephone companies to offer better and less expensive long-distance service. Today, people can call friends overseas for less money than it would take to buy a meal at a fast-food restaurant.

A global network of dependable telephone service was necessary before the Internet could come into existence. Because of the Internet, people in industrialized nations all over the world can now exchange e-mail, pictures, music, and other data in a matter of seconds. This high-speed connection allows online business ventures, as well as personal friendship and family connections, to flourish.

Historian Dawne M. Flammger said:

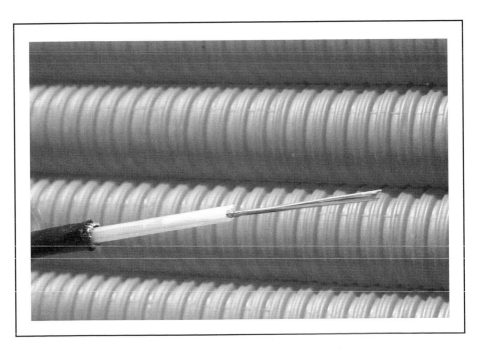

Fiber-optic cables revolutionized the telephone business.

the invention of the telephone has resulted in the rapid and diffuse dissemination of technical and scientific information, saved lives through links to emergency services, made possible the modern city through telephonic connections, increased the speed and ease with which information changes place, and accelerated the rate of scientific and technological change and growth in industry.[8]

The Future of Telecommunications

While no one can predict what the future may hold, we can be sure that scientists and inventors are working

This microwave transmitting tower, used by the military, is an example of how far communications have come.

on faster and better ways of communicating by means of electrical impulses.

So what will be next? Will cellular phones get even smaller? Will we surf the Internet on a computer no thicker than a piece of notebook paper? Will it be possible to download movies and television shows over the Internet in a matter of seconds? Will people on Earth hear broadcasts from space stations on Mars or the moons of Jupiter? Will the governments of the world permit free communication? Or will the fear of terrorism cause political leaders to cut back on the rights to communicate that Americans already have?

Tom Standage, author of *The Victorian Internet: The Remarkable Story of the Telegraph and the Nineteenth Century's Online Pioneers*, wrote:

> Given a new invention, there will always be some people who see only its potential to do good, while others see new opportunities to commit crime or make money. We can expect exactly the same reactions to whatever new inventions appear in the twenty-first century.[9]

★ TIMELINE ★

1837—Charles Wheatstone patents what he calls the "electric telegraph."

1843—Morse convinces Congress to fund the first telegraph line between Washington, D.C., and Baltimore, Maryland.

1844—Samuel F. B. Morse demonstrates his telegraph by sending a message to Baltimore from the chambers of the Supreme Court in Washington, D.C.

1845—The Magnetic Telegraph Company goes into business.

1847—The telegraph is first used as a business tool.

1850—Morse patents the "clicking telegraph."

1855—The printing telegraph is first used in the United States.

1856—On April 4, The New York & Mississippi Valley Printing Telegraph Company officially changes the name of its union of thirteen different companies to "Western Union."

1858—The transatlantic cable is placed in the Atlantic Ocean, but problems soon limit its usefulness; Soon after, no telegraphic communication can be sent between the United States and Europe.

1861—On October 21, Western Union joins wires from the East with wires from the West at Salt Lake City, completing the first transcontinental telegraph; The Pony Express horseback message service comes to an abrupt end when a telegraph line connects California to the East.

1867—The New York Stock Exchange starts using stock tickers.

1868—An ocean vessel called the *Great Eastern* lays the first transatlantic cable that works for more than a month.

1869—On May 10, the Union Pacific and Central Pacific tracks meet at Promontory, Utah, to complete a transcontinental railroad; News of the event is relayed across the nation by means of telegraph.

1872—On April 2, Samuel Morse dies in New York; Western Electric Manufacturing Co. starts to manufacture their own telegraph instruments.

1875—Alexander Graham Bell makes his first transmission of sound by telephone.

1876—Bell obtains a patent for the telephone and demonstrates his invention at the Philadelphia Centennial Exhibition.

1877—The Bell Telephone Company is established.

1878—The first telephone directories that list customers are issued.

1880s—Home and business telephone service is available in most eastern cities.

1884—In some parts of the country, people are able to make long-distance phone calls through an operator.

1896—The first dial telephones are put into use.

1904—The telephone answering machine is invented.

1915—The transcontinental telephone service connects New York to San Francisco, California.

★ CHAPTER NOTES ★

Chapter 1. A New Invention

1. Ernest Victor Heyn, *Fire of Genius: Inventors of the Past Century Based on the Files of* Popular Science Monthly *Since Its Founding in 1872* (Garden City, N.Y.: Anchor Press/Doubleday, 1976), p. 57.

Chapter 2. Learning About the Power of Electricity

1. Beverley Eyre, *Benjamin Franklin*, February 8, 1999, <http://www.ee.ucla.edu/~eyre/people/franklin2.html> (March 14, 2003).

2. John H. Lienhard, "Faraday and Magnetism," *Engines of Our Ingenuity*, ©1988–2000, <http://www.uh.edu/engines/epi1613.htm> (March 14, 2003).

Chapter 3. Samuel Morse Invents the Telegraph

1. "Chappe Innovation and Politics in 1793 and 1794," *The Optical Telegraph*, n.d., <http://www.telemuseum.se/historia/optel/otsymp/Frankrike.html> (May 6, 2003).

2. L. Sprague De Camp, *The Heroic Age of American Invention* (New York: Doubleday & Company, Inc, 1961), pp. 67–68.

3. Carlton Mabee, *American Leonardo—A Life of Samuel F. B. Morse* (New York: Octagon Books, 1969), p. 154.

4. David Lindsay, *Madness in the Making: The Triumphant Rise & Ultimate Fall of America's Show Inventors* (New York: Kodansha America, Inc., 1997), p. 95.

5. Ibid., p. 96.

6. Joseph and Frances Gies, *The Ingenious Yankees* (New York: Thomas Y. Crowell Company, 1976), p. 219.

7. Mabee, p. 248.

8. Ibid., p. 251.

9. Gies and Gies, p. 221.

10. Phil Ault, *Wires West, the Story of the Talking Wires* (New York: Dodd, Mead & Company, 1974), p. 15.

11. Ibid., p. 15.

12. "Journal of the House of Representatives of the United States, 1842–1843," Library of Congress, February 23, 1843, <http://lcweb2.loc.gov/cgi/bin/query/D?hlaw:11:./temp/~ammem_G9U2::> (March 14, 2003).

13. Gies and Gies, p. 221.

14. Tom Standage, *The Victorian Internet: The Remarkable Story of the Telegraph and the Nineteenth Century's On-line Pioneers* (New York: Berkley Books, 1999), p. 47.

15. Ault, p. 16.

16. "Caution: Telegraph in Use," *The Once and Future Web*, n.d., <http://www.nlm.nih.gov/onceandfutureweb/database/secb/case3.html> (May 6, 2003).

Chapter 4. How the Telegraph Changed America

1. "The Once and Future Web," *National Library of Medicine*, n.d.,<http://www.nlm.nih.gov/onceandfutureweb/database/seca/case3.html> (March 14, 2003).

2. Tom Standage, *The Victorian Internet: The Remarkable Story of the Telegraph and the Nineteenth Century's On-line Pioneers* (New York: Berkley Books, 1999), pp. 57–58.

3. Ibid., p. 57.

4. Phil Ault, *Wires West, the Story of the Talking Wires* (New York: Dodd, Mead & Company, 1974), p. 58.

5. Ibid., p. 60.

6. Patti Norton, "The Aurora Borealis and the Telegraph," *Rainbow Riders' Trading Post*, n.d., <http://www.rainbowriderstradingpost.com/article1.html> (March 14, 2003).

7. Virginia Penny, *How Women Can Make Money* (Springfield, Mass.: Fisk & Co., 1870), p. 101.

8. "The Once and Future Web," *National Library of Medicine*, n.d., <http://www.nlm.nih.gov/onceandfutureweb/database/secb/case2.html> (March 14, 2003).

9. L. C. Hall, "Telegraph Talk and Talkers," *McClure's*, January 1902, pp. 227–231.

10. "The Once and Future Web," *National Library of Medicine*, n.d., <http://www.nlm.nih.gov/onceandfutureweb/database/secb/case2.html> (March 14, 2003).

11. Matthew Josephson, *Edison: A Biography* (New York: McGraw-Hill Book Company, 1959), p. 25.

12. Ibid.

13. "Carnegie Started as a Bobbin Boy," *The New York Times*, 2001, <http://www.nytimes.com/learning/general/onthisday/bday/1125.html> (March 14, 2003).

14. Joseph and Frances Gies, *The Ingenious Yankees* (New York: Thomas Y. Crowell Company, 1976), p. 224.

15. Debra K. Fly, "The End," *The Pony Express*, n.d., <http://www.unomaha.edu/~wwwsped/spd/apl/def/lsn/5/info.html> (March 14, 2003).

16. Standage, p. 40.

17. Stephen Ambrose, *Nothing Like It in the World: The Men Who Built the Transcontinental Railroad, 1863–1869* (New York: Simon & Schuster, 2000), p. 370.

Chapter 5. The Telephone Enters American Life

1. Michael E. Gorman, "3.9 Bell's Ear Mental Model," *Invention and Discovery: A Cognitive Quest*, 1997,

<http://www.iath.virginia.edu/~meg3c/id/TCC313/ear. html> (March 14, 2003).

2. *Alexander Graham Bell—A Tribute to the Inventor of the Telephone on the One Hundredth Anniversary of his Birth 1847–1947* (New York: AT&T, 1947), p. 22.

3. Alexander Graham Bell, "Letter from Alexander Graham Bell to Mabel Hubbard Bell, June 21, 1876," *Library of Congress: American Memory,* n.d., <http:// memory.loc.gov> (May 6, 2003).

4. *Alexander Graham Bell—A Tribute to the Inventor of the Telephone on the One Hundredth Anniversary of his Birth 1847–1947,* p. 24.

5. Robert W. Bruce, *Bell: Alexander Graham Bell and the Conquest of Solitude* (Boston: Little, Brown, & Company, 1973), p. 210.

6. Charles Moran, "We Write, But Do We Read?", *Computers and Composition,* August 1991, pp. 51–61, <http://corax.cwrl.utexas.edu/cac/archives/v8/8_3_html/ 8_3_4_Moran.html> (March 17, 2003).

7. Jacques Leslie, *From Fire to "Flames,"* 1998, <http://www.well.com/user/jacques/fromfiretoflames. html> (March 17, 2003).

8. John Brooks, *Telephone: The First Hundred Years* (New York: Harper & Row, 1975), p. 65.

9. "Number Please," *Technology in 1900,* n.d., <http://www.pbs.org/wgbh/amex/kids/tech1900/phone. html> (March 17, 2003).

10. Phil Ault, *Wires West, the Story of the Talking Wires* (New York: Dodd, Mead & Company, 1974), p. 151.

11. "Lecture 9: Developing a Phone System," n.d., <http://www.chass.utoronto.ca/~bhall/hps282f/LECTU RE%209%20Telephone%20System.htm> (March 17, 2003).

12. "Article, October 15, 1879," *Library of Congress: American Memory,* n.d., <http://memory.loc.gov> (May 6, 2003).

13. "Talking Wires: The Development of the Telephone," © 2000–2001, <http://www.moah.org/exhibits/archives/talkingwires.html> (March 17, 2003).

14. "A Brief History," *AT&T, 2003*, <http://www.att.com/history/history1.html> (March 13, 2003).

15. Jeff Garber, "Phones and Culture," n.d., <http://www.pensive.org/jeff/mrfone/culture.htm> (March 17, 2003).

16. "Milestones in Women's History," IM Diversity.com, 2002, <http://www.imdiversity.com/Article_Detail.asp?Article_ID=3434> (March 17, 2003).

17. Herbert N. Casson, "The History of the Telephone," *Telephone Tribute.com*, 1910, <http://www.telephonetribute.com/tribute/the_history_of_the_telephone.html> (March 17, 2003).

Chapter 6. America Gets Connected

1. *Alexander Graham Bell—A Tribute to the Inventor of the Telephone on the One Hundredth Anniversary of his Birth 1847–1947* (New York: AT&T, 1947), p. 24.

2. Phil Ault, *Wires West, The Story of the Talking Wires* (New York: Dodd, Mead & Company, 1974), p. 163.

3. Nelson E. Ross, "How to Write Telegrams Properly," *The Telegraph Office*, 1928, <http://www.metronet.com/~nmcewen/telegram.html> (March 17, 2003).

4. "Fire Alarm Telegraph and Electric Police Patrol Systems," *Adventures in Cybersound*, n.d., <http://www.acmi.net.au/AIC/TELEGRAPHY_LULA.html

5. Claude S. Fischer, *America Calling: A Social History of the Telephone to 1940* (Berkeley: University of California Press, 1994), p. 2.

6. "Housekeeper Objects to Telephone Advertising," *Telephony*, February 20, 1909, <http://www.ipass.net/~whitetho/1909ads.htm> (March 17, 2003).

7. "Telephone Service," *Fargo, North Dakota*, n.d., <http://www.fargo-history.com/utilities/telephone.htm> (March 17, 2003).

8. Dawne M. Flammger, *A History of the Telephone*, February 1, 1995, <http://www.geog.buffalo.edu/Geo666/flammger/tele2.html> (2001).

9. Tom Standage, *The Victorian Internet: The Remarkable Story of the Telegraph and the Nineteenth Century's On-line Pioneers* (New York: Berkley Books, 1999), p. 212.

★ FURTHER READING ★

Gan, Geraldine. *Communication*. Broomall, Pa.: Chelsea House, 1997.

Gearhart, Sarah. *The Telephone*. New York: Simon & Schuster, 1999.

Henderson, Harry. *Communications and Broadcasting*. New York: Facts On File, 1997.

Kerby, Mona. *Samuel Morse*. New York: Franklin Watts, 1991.

Kozar, Richard. *Inventors and Their Discoveries*. Broomall, Pa.: Chelsea House, 1999.

Lampton, Christopher. *Telecommunications: From Telegraphs to Modems*. New York: Franklin Watts, 1991.

Parker, Steve. *Alexander Graham Bell and the Telephone*. Broomall, Pa.: Chelsea House, 1995.

Schuman, Michael A. *Alexander Graham Bell, Inventor and Teacher*. Berkeley Heights, N.J.: Enslow Publishers, Inc., 1999.

Standage, Tom. *The Victorian Internet: The Remarkable Story of the Telegraph and the Nineteenth Century's On-line Pioneers*. New York: Berkley Books, 1999.

Streissguth, Thomas. *Communications: Sending the Message*. Minneapolis, Minn.: Oliver Press, Inc., 1997.

Tames, Richard. *Alexander Graham Bell*. New York: Franklin Watts, 1990.

Weaver, Robyn M. *The Alexander Graham Bell*. Farmington Hills, Mich.: Gale Group, 1999.

Webb, Marcus. *Telephones: Words over Wires*. Farmington Hills, Mich.: Gale Group, 1992.

★ Internet Addresses ★

Mary Bellis. "The History of the Telegraph and Telegraphy." *About.com*. 2003. <http://inventors. about.com/library/inventors/bltelegraph.htm>.

Telecomwriting.com. n.d. <http://www.privateline. com/>.

William von Alven. "Bill's 200-Year Condensed History of Telecommunications." *Communication Certification Laboratory*. May 1998. <http:// www.cclab.com/billhist.htm>.

★ INDEX ★